BAJC

OCT -- 2022

This book belongs to:

....

 | Penguin Random House

Senior Editors Dawn Sirett, Lizzie Munsey
Art Editor Polly Appleton
Text by Andrea Mills, Ben Hubbard
Subject Consultant Dr. Jonathan Dale
Designed by Hannah Moore, Rhys Thomas, Sadie Thomas
US Senior Editor Shannon Beatty
US Editor Mindy Fichter
Additional Illustrations Kitty Glavin
Project Picture Researcher Sakshi Saluja
Senior Production Editor Nikoleta Parasaki
Production Controller John Casey
Jacket Designer Sadie Thomas
Jacket Coordinator Issy Walsh
Managing Editor Penny Smith
Deputy Art Director Mabel Chan
Publishing Director Sarah Larter

First American Edition, 2022
Published in the United States by DK Publishing
1745 Broadway, 20th Floor, New York NY 10019

Copyright © 2022 Dorling Kindersley Limited
DK, a Division of Penguin Random House LLC
22 23 24 25 26 10 9 8 7 6 5 4 3 2 1
001–325875–Oct/2022

A catalog record for this book is available from the Library of Congress.
ISBN 978-0-7440-5973-1

DK books are available at special discounts when purchased in bulk
for sales promotions, premiums, fund-raising, or educational use.
For details, contact:
DK Publishing Special Markets,
1745 Broadway, 20th Floor, New York NY 10019
SpecialSales@dk.com

Printed and bound in China

For the curious
www.dk.com

MIX
Paper | Supporting
responsible forestry
FSC™ C018179

This book was made with Forest
Stewardship Council™ certified
paper–one small step in DK's
commitment to a sustainable
future. For more information go to
www.dk.com/our-green-pledge

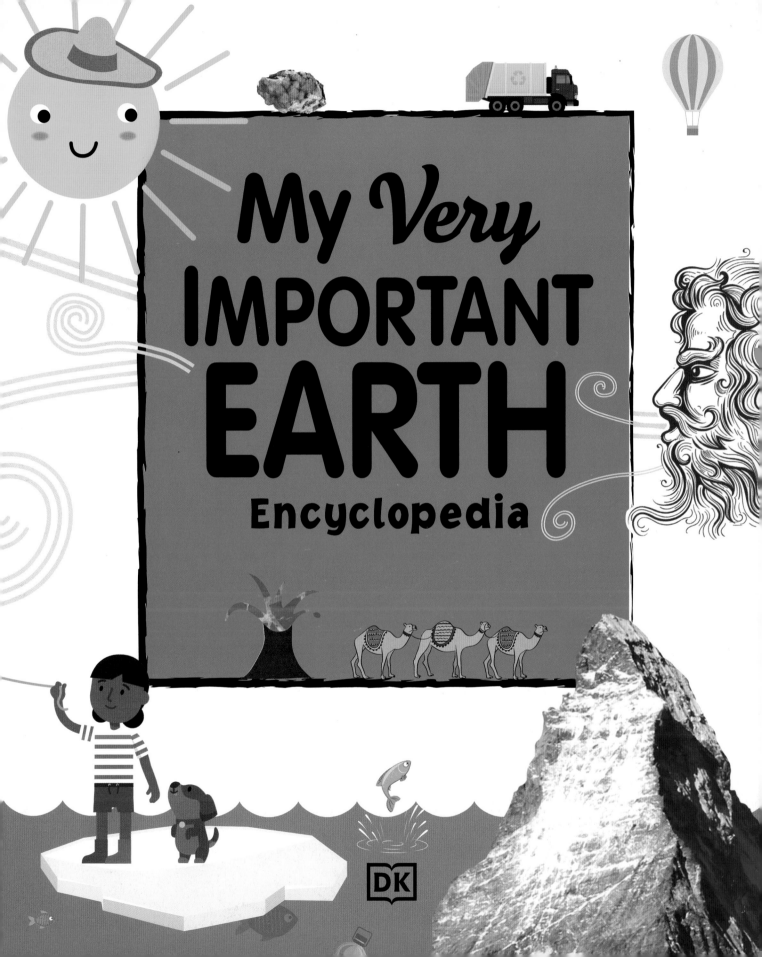

My Very IMPORTANT EARTH Encyclopedia

DK

Contents

Weather

Habitats

Human planet

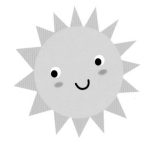

Save our planet!

Our Earth

Get ready for an **around-the-world adventure**. Gaze at the starriest skies, journey to the fiery center of our world, visit the ocean floor, and climb the highest mountains. Explore Planet Earth and discover the amazing subject of **geography**.

Where are we?

Our wonderful world is a **big**, **beautiful rock** spinning in outer space. Planet Earth is the only place in the entire universe where **life** is known to exist.

Earth

Earth is home to almost eight billion people, including you!

Planet Earth

Earth is the only planet known to have **liquid water**. In fact, more than 70 percent of its surface is ocean. The rest is land, with amazing landscapes of deserts, mountains, and forests.

Torres del Paine National Park, Chile

The solar system

The sun

Earth is the **third planet** from the sun.

The solar system

Planet Earth is in a part of space called the solar system. Earth is one of **eight planets** in the solar system, which all travel around the **sun**. One of **billions of stars** in the universe, the sun is a fiery ball of gas.

The Milky Way

The solar system is one of many such systems in outer space.

The universe

Everything that exists is part of the universe. Earth means the world to us, but it is only a tiny part of the universe.

Galaxies

There are **billions** of galaxies in the universe. Each one is made up of countless **stars** and **planets**, as well as **gas** and **dust**. Earth is in the **Milky Way galaxy**.

Galaxies

Looking **out**

Turn your eyes to the skies for a
spectacular surprise!

On a clear night, the view from
Earth includes the moon, twinkling stars,
pinprick planets, and circling satellites.

The moon is the easiest object to spot in the night sky. The moon doesn't make its own light, but appears to shine because its surface reflects sunlight.

SAFETY NOTE: Remember, when looking at the sky in the daytime, don't look directly at the sun, and NEVER look at the sun through a telescope or binoculars.

Telescopes

Astronomers and stargazers look
through telescopes to make
distant space objects
appear **closer** and **bigger**.

From Earth, you can see around 5,000

Aquarius   **Scorpius**   **Sagittarius**   **Capricornus**

Constellations

For thousands of years, astronomers have linked stars in the sky into **pictures** called constellations. These imaginary pictures can be of people, animals, or objects. There are eighty-eight constellations altogether.

Circling Earth are thousands of satellites, which were launched into orbit by rockets. They carry out tasks such as checking the weather and connecting cell phones.

There are other planets beyond our solar system, but they are too dark for us to see.

Planets

The brightest planets in the night sky are **Jupiter**, **Mars**, **Mercury**, **Saturn**, and **Venus**. They can be seen from Earth and change position in the night sky depending on the time of year.

This is a view of Venus through a telescope—showing as a crescent.

stars without even using a telescope.

Orion the hunter

In the starry skies, a man goes hunting every night. This is **Orion**, a **hero of ancient Greek mythology**. He is one of the brightest and best-known **constellations**.

Orion has more bright stars than any other constellation. Its two brightest stars are called Betelgeuse and Rigel.

Betelgeuse

Read on for the story of Orion!

Orion's Belt
Three stars that create a short line in the constellation are called Orion's Belt.

Rigel

The myth of Orion

Orion was the son of the sea god Poseidon. He grew into a **fearless hunter**.

Orion   Poseidon

Orion hunted animals using his unbreakable club. But over time, he boasted too much about his power, saying he would kill all creatures.

Gaia, the Goddess of Earth, did not like what Orion was saying. She wanted to protect the animals and sent a scorpion to kill Orion.

A battle took place, ending when the scorpion's tail delivered a deadly sting. Orion died instantly, but his legend lives on in the night sky.

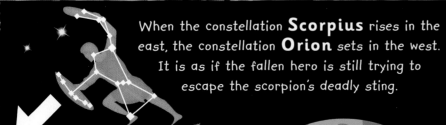

When the constellation **Scorpius** rises in the east, the constellation **Orion** sets in the west. It is as if the fallen hero is still trying to escape the scorpion's deadly sting.

West

East

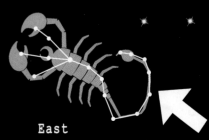

Around the sun

The **sun** is the **star** at the center of our **solar system**. It's a superhot ball of glowing gas. Eight **planets**, as well as **comets** and **asteroids**, travel around it.

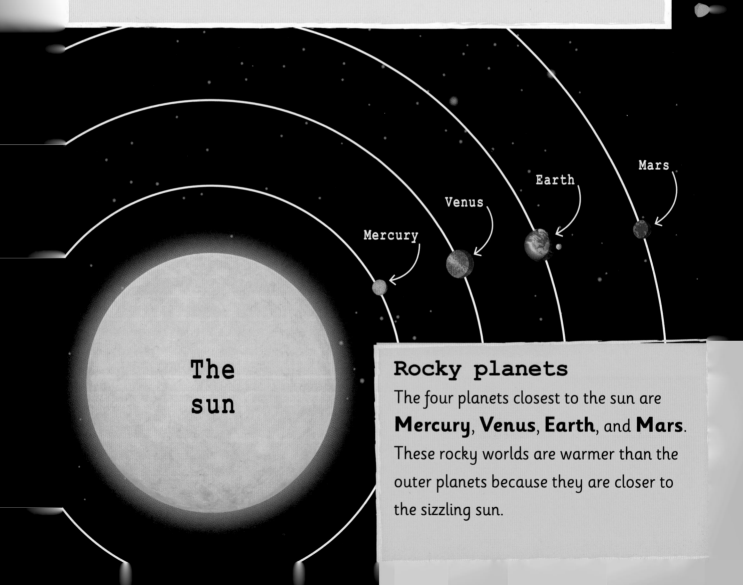

The sun

Mercury

Venus

Earth

Mars

Rocky planets
The four planets closest to the sun are **Mercury**, **Venus**, **Earth**, and **Mars**. These rocky worlds are warmer than the outer planets because they are closer to the sizzling sun.

Shooting stars are actually small space rocks, called meteors. They burn up and glow as they fall into the air around Earth.

Gas planets

The outer planets, **Jupiter**, **Saturn**, **Uranus**, and **Neptune**, are enormous and made of gas and liquid. Some have huge rings of dust and icy rock around them.

Neptune

Uranus

Saturn

Jupiter

Asteroid belt

Thousands of **space rocks** called **asteroids** orbit the sun between Mars and Jupiter. They form the asteroid belt.

Trillions of comets travel around the sun. A comet is an icy object, as big as a city, and with a tail of gas and dust. Comets are a little bit like huge snowballs!

Spinning Earth

Our planet is a great little mover!
It **spins constantly**
on its own axis and
around the sun.

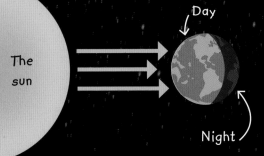

Day

The
sun

Night

Direction of spin

Earth's axis

Earth is like a **spinning
top**, rotating around a
slightly tilted axis. The
part of Earth that faces the sun
has day, while the part facing
away from the sun has night. Our
planet takes **24 hours**—one day
and one night—to complete one spin.

Earth's orbit

Earth's orbit is the **route** it takes around the sun. It takes Earth **365 days**— a whole year—to complete its journey around the sun.

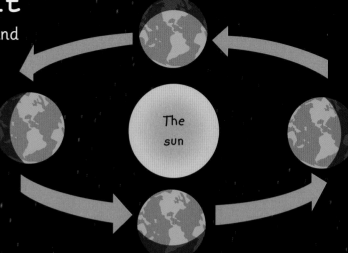

The sun

Superspeeds

Earth spins and orbits around the sun at top speeds. So, why don't we get **dizzy**? Because these **speeds always stay the same**. Our planet never starts to move faster or slower, so we can't feel it moving. Phew!

Imagine how dizzy we would *be* if we could feel Earth spinning!

The sun is around one million times bigger than Earth.

The moon

Most nights, the silvery moon shines down on you. Although this instantly recognizable **rock** looks very close, it would take you **three days** to get there in a spaceship. **Zoom**!

Making the moon

The moon was made around 4.5 billion years ago when the partly-formed, early Earth was smashed up in a **space collision**. Pieces of rock came together to make Earth as we know it today and the moon.

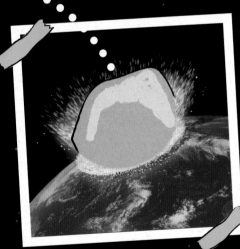

Space collision

Meet the moon

The moon is a **cold**, **dry rock** around four times smaller than Earth.

Moon pal

The moon is a great friend to Earth. It travels around our planet every **27 days** and comes with us on our **yearly trip** around the sun.

The moon

Earth

Look out for new space trips to the moon, such as the Artemis missions.

Walking on the moon

The moon is the only place people have visited beyond Earth. The first people to walk on the moon were the **Apollo 11 astronauts** Neil Armstrong and Buzz Aldrin, in 1969.

Buzz Aldrin stepping onto the moon

The moon has fascinated people for thousands of years. Some say a full moon (the complete circle phase) can turn people into werewolves!

HOOOWWWWl!

Phases of the moon

As the moon travels around Earth, the **different amounts of sunlight** that hit it make it seem to **change shape**. These changing shapes are called the **phases** of the moon.

Seasons

Many places on Earth have four seasons. These spectacular seasons affect **all aspects of nature**, from the weather to plants and animals. They are created by our planet tilting.

Earth's tilt

A long time ago, Earth was struck by a **space rock**. This big hit pushed our planet, causing it to **tilt** at an **angle**. This means that different parts of Earth experience different levels of sunlight, which causes the seasons.

Tropical zone

South Pole

The four seasons are a repeating cycle of

Spring

Summer

North Pole

The equator

When the northern part of Earth tilts toward the sun, it is summer there.

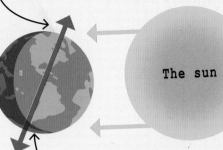

The sun

When the southern part of Earth tilts away from the sun, it is winter there.

Changing seasons

Earth's tilt means that **one half** of our planet is always **closer** to the sun than the other. The two halves experience **different seasons** as Earth travels around the sun.

Middle ground

The **equator** is an imaginary line around the middle of Earth. The places at and near the equator, in the **tropical zone**, do not have four seasons. They get the same amount of sunlight all year, and are hot and stormy all year round or have only wet and dry seasons.

The areas at Earth's North and South poles have summers and winters, but they stay icy cold throughout the year.

SPRING, SUMMER, FALL, and WINTER.

Fall

Winter

Inside the Earth

When you're digging on a beach, do you wonder where you might end up? Don't worry! Inside Earth there are so many **layers of rock** and **metal** you could never dig past them.

Earth's layers

Our planet is like an **onion**—it has many layers! The ground beneath our feet is just the very top layer.

Let's journey to the center of the Earth!

Crust

We all live on Earth's crust—a **thin layer of solid rock**. There are two types of crust, continental crust under the land and oceanic crust under the seas.

Mantle

Under the crust is the very slow-moving mantle. This layer is **mostly superhot, solid rock**, but **some parts of it** are **liquid rock**, called **magma**.

Outer core

The outer core is made of **liquid metal**, which rushes around as Earth spins, creating a **magnetic field** around our planet. The magnetic field protects us from dangerous particles in outer space.

Inner core

The very center of Earth is a **great ball of solid metal**. It is scorching hot here, with temperatures as high as those on the surface of the sun.

The air around us

Although you can't see it, Earth is surrounded by **layers of gas** called the **atmosphere.** This is a protective shield for our planet—it absorbs harmful rays from the sun and creates a temperature that is safe for us to live in.

Satellite

Exosphere

The **top layer** of Earth's atmosphere blends into outer space. There is very little gas here and the air is **too thin** to breathe.

Thermosphere

This **vast expanse** of atmosphere is where the **polar lights** put on their dazzling shows. These natural light displays happen around Earth's North and South poles.

Polar lights

Layers of the atmosphere

Earth's atmosphere is divided into **five layers.** The air in the atmosphere becomes thinner as it gets higher and farther away from Earth's surface.

Mesosphere

Shooting stars fly through the air here. The mesosphere is also the **coldest section** of Earth's atmosphere.

Shooting stars are pieces of space rock burning up in the atmosphere.

Ultraviolet rays

Stratosphere

This is home to the **ozone layer**, which absorbs most of the dangerous ultraviolet rays from the sun, protecting life on Earth. Aircraft fly here.

Ozone layer

Troposphere

This is the **air you breathe.** The **weather** takes place here—there are puffy clouds and falling rain.

Without the atmosphere, Earth would be too cold for people to survive. Brrrr!

27

Earth in pieces

Earth's crust is like a giant **jigsaw puzzle** made up of enormous flat pieces of rock. The **pieces** of this puzzle move around, changing the surface of our planet.

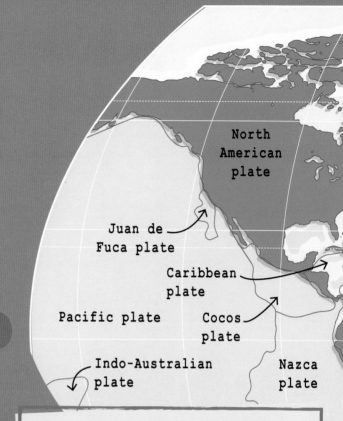

North American plate

Juan de Fuca plate

Caribbean plate

Pacific plate

Cocos plate

Indo-Australian plate

Nazca plate

Tectonic plates
The **pieces** that make up Earth's crust are called tectonic plates. They **move**, but very **slowly**.

Plate boundaries
The areas where the **edges of tectonic plates meet** are called plate boundaries. The plate edges can meet and interact with each other in three different ways.

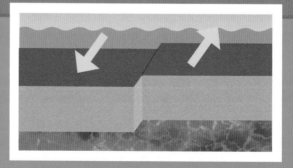

Rubbing along
Two plates may meet and rub together. The energy between the two can cause powerful earthquakes, experienced as shaky ground on Earth's surface.

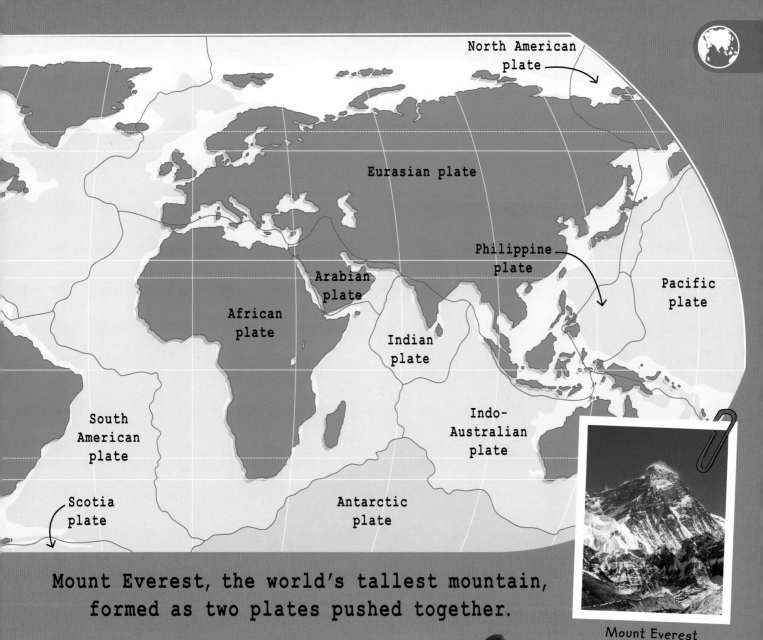

North American plate

Eurasian plate

Philippine plate

Pacific plate

Arabian plate

African plate

Indian plate

Indo-Australian plate

South American plate

Scotia plate

Antarctic plate

Mount Everest, the world's tallest mountain, formed as two plates pushed together.

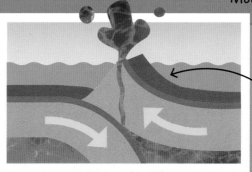

Mount Everest

Pulling apart

Two plates may pull apart from each other, leaving a gap between them. If this happens under the sea, then the ocean floor expands.

Volcanoes can form when plates push together.

Pushing together

Two plates may crash into one another. One plate is pushed above the other, making mountains and volcanoes on Earth's surface.

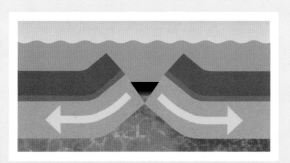

Land on the move

Although you can't feel it, **Earth's tectonic plates** are **moving** slowly and constantly. Over millions of years, this slow movement has changed our world dramatically.

Plate tectonics

Tectonic plates drift across the Earth. These **slow-moving slabs** carry landmasses on top of them. This means that over time, **continents move around** and the **oceans** can get **bigger** or **smaller**.

Studying the history of our planet and looking at its physical features is called geology. The scientists who do this are called geologists.

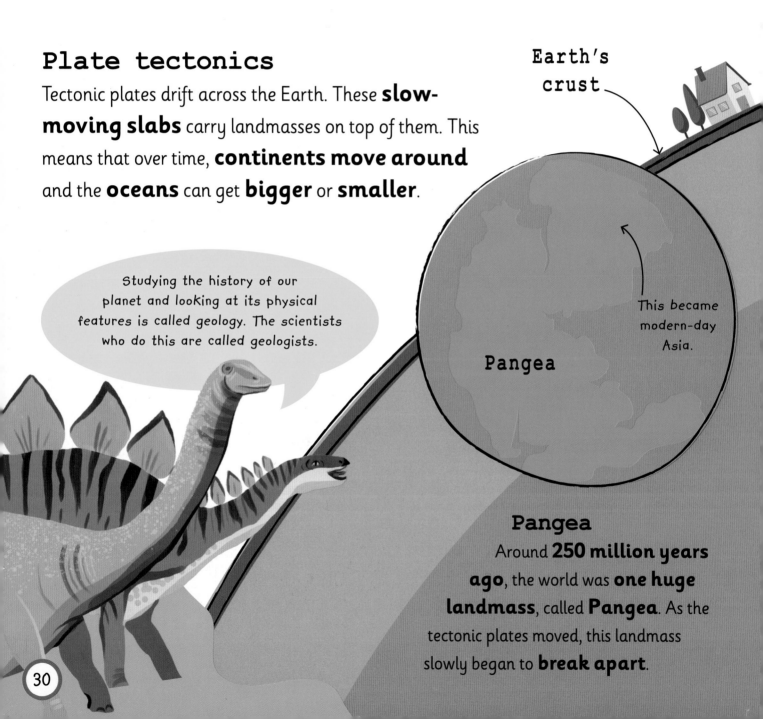

Earth's crust

This became modern-day Asia.

Pangea

Pangea
Around **250 million years ago**, the world was **one huge landmass**, called **Pangea**. As the tectonic plates moved, this landmass slowly began to **break apart**.

Powered by heat

Tectonic plate movement is powered by **heat currents** in the mantle layer of Earth. This heat **moves plates** along slowly and constantly.

Tectonic plates move at around the same speed as your fingernails grow.

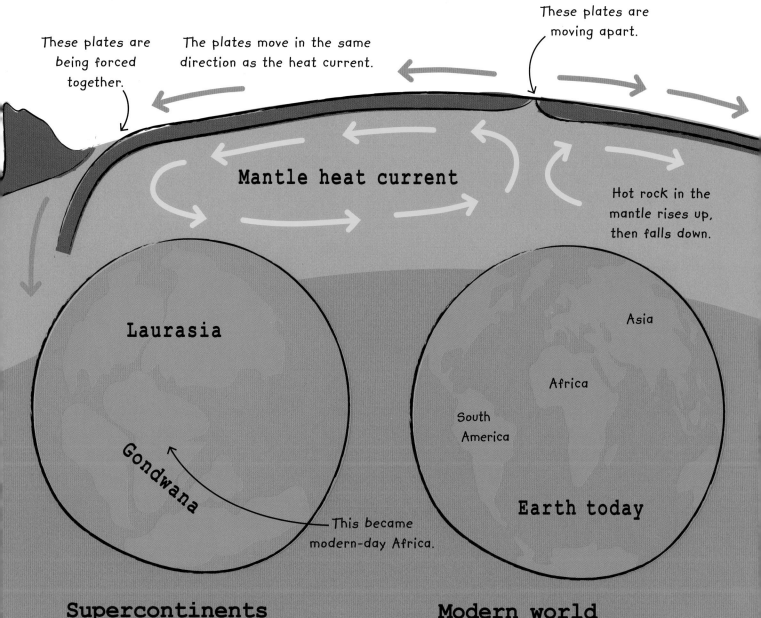

These plates are being forced together.

The plates move in the same direction as the heat current.

These plates are moving apart.

Mantle heat current

Hot rock in the mantle rises up, then falls down.

Laurasia

Gondwana

This became modern-day Africa.

Asia

Africa

South America

Earth today

Supercontinents

Around **200 million years ago**, when dinosaurs roamed the Earth, Pangea broke into **two great supercontinents**, which we call **Laurasia** and **Gondwana**.

Modern world

Around **65 million years ago**, the tectonic plates **spread out** across the globe, forming the **continents** we recognize today.

The ocean floor

The ocean floor is an **underwater wonderland** of volcanoes, mountains, ridges, and trenches. New features are created as Earth's tectonic plates move around and the oceans change shape.

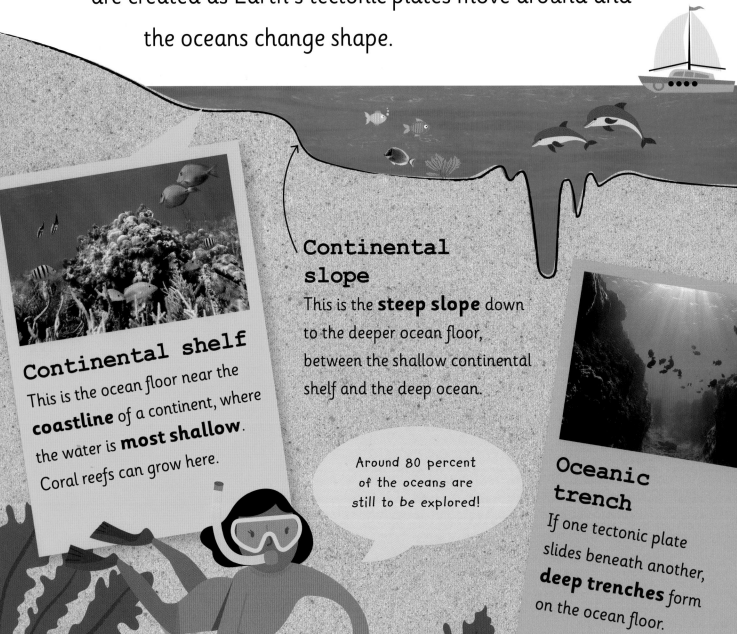

Continental slope

This is the **steep slope** down to the deeper ocean floor, between the shallow continental shelf and the deep ocean.

Continental shelf

This is the ocean floor near the **coastline** of a continent, where the water is **most shallow**. Coral reefs can grow here.

Around 80 percent of the oceans are still to be explored!

Oceanic trench

If one tectonic plate slides beneath another, **deep trenches** form on the ocean floor.

Mariana Trench

The **deepest location** on Earth's surface is the Mariana Trench in the Pacific Ocean. The bottom of this trench is **deeper than Mount Everest is tall**.

Guyot
This is a seamount with a **flat top**.

Volcanic island
A volcano tall enough to break through the surface of the sea can form a **volcanic island**.

Seamount
Volcanic eruptions on the seabed create **underwater mountains**, called seamounts.

Oceanic ridge
An oceanic ridge is a **long**, **narrow ridge** on the ocean floor, similar to a mountain range on land.

Earthquakes

A sudden **shaking** of the ground is the result of tectonic plates **moving**. Earthquakes range from tiny tremors that you can barely feel to colossal shakes that cause **destruction** and **devastation**.

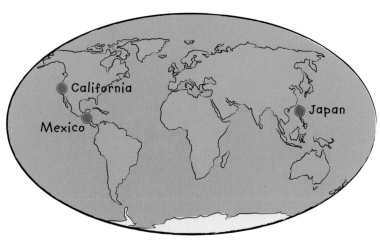

California

Mexico

Japan

Finding the fault

A **fault line** is a place where tectonic plates meet. The most active fault lines in the world are located in **Japan**, **Mexico**, and **California**.

More than one million earthquakes shake our planet every year.

How do earthquakes happen?

On the ground above the focus, is the epicenter. This is where the earthquake shakes the most and makes the biggest impact.

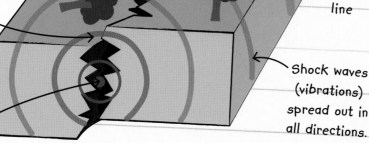

Fault line

Shock waves (vibrations) spread out in all directions.

The focus of an earthquake is where the pressure builds up.

The above example shows two tectonic plates moving sideways. Earthquakes also happen when two tectonic plates slide upward or downward past each other.

1. Two tectonic plates get **stuck together** and cannot slide past each other.

2. Over time, **pressure** begins to build at the point where the plates are stuck.

3. The plates **move suddenly**, and the **vibrations** reach the land above.

Craaaaack!

Eeeek! I'm out of here.

Moonquakes are earthquakes that happen on the moon!

Living with earthquakes

Luckily, not many earthquakes make a big impact. But some cause great **destruction**. Scientists measure the **size** of earthquakes to understand them, and there are things we can do that help us live with earthquakes.

Seismograph

This machine measures the force of an earthquake by recording the power of its vibrations.

Moment magnitude scale

This scale is used to **measure the energy** of earthquakes. The higher the number on the scale, the more powerful the earthquake. There are other scales, such as the **Richter scale**, but they are less accurate for large earthquakes.

Moment magnitude scale	Less than 3.5	3.5–5.4	5.5–6.0
	Weak earthquake, only recorded by geologists	Earthquake makes the ground shake, but causes little damage	Earthquake destroys weaker buildings

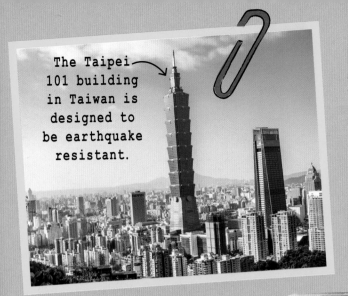

The Taipei 101 building in Taiwan is designed to be earthquake resistant.

Earthquake-proof buildings

Buildings can be designed to limit the impact of earthquakes on them. For example, **rubber pads** in the foundations act as shock absorbers, and **steel bars** make buildings sturdy and stop them from moving too much.

Safety at school

In countries where earthquakes happen, children attend **safety classes** to learn what to do in an emergency. The advice is to **shelter under a table** if you are indoors, or **move away from buildings and trees** if you are outside.

I'll come out once the shaking has stopped!

6.1–6.9	7.0–7.9	8 or greater
Destruction across a wider community	Big earthquake, causing major damage	Huge earthquake, capable of destroying cities

Tsunamis

Tsunamis are **giant ocean waves**. They move fast and can cause disaster on land. A tsunami can be triggered by an underwater earthquake, a volcanic eruption, or a coastal or underwater landslide (earth or rocks sliding down a slope).

The biggest tsunami ever recorded was a wave in Alaska. It was the same height as five Statues of Liberty.

Making waves

A tsunami forms as a result of a **disturbance**, such as an underwater earthquake.

Most tsunamis happen in the Pacific Ocean.

Tsunamis can travel as fast as

Tsunami alert

Detection systems can help to predict tsunamis. **Sensors** placed on the ocean floor check for **vibrations** caused by earthquakes and volcanoes. Experts can then warn people about any unusual activity.

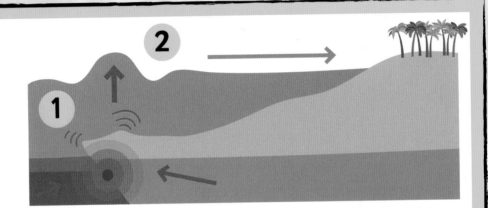

1. An earthquake shakes the seabed, which forces water toward the surface.

2. Waves move toward the shore at high speed.

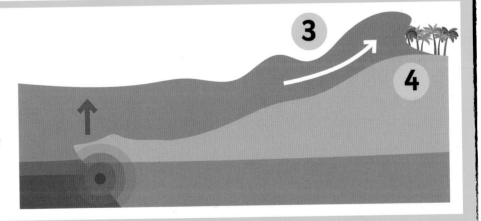

3. Huge waves peak in shallow water and flood the coastline.

4. The tsunami damages anything it hits, including buildings and roads.

an airplane!

Volcanoes

BLAST! Volcanoes release melted rock, hot ash, and toxic gases from deep inside the Earth in **explosive eruptions**.

Erupting Earth

Volcanoes form where hot, liquid rock called **magma** explodes onto Earth's surface. Magma that reaches the surface is called **lava**. Hot, liquid lava flows over the ground, while ash and gases escape into the air.

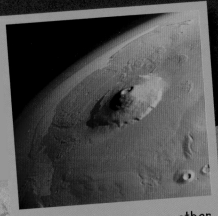

There are volcanoes on other planets. Mars is home to Olympus Mons, the largest volcano in the solar system.

The main vent is the biggest opening in the volcano.

Side vents are small openings on the sides of a volcano.

The magma chamber is full of superhot, melted rock.

Thick clouds of ash and gases form above the volcano.

Melted rock called lava bursts out of the volcano.

Lava bombs are pieces of hot rock that fly through the air.

Dead or alive?

Extinct volcanoes are not expected to erupt ever again.

Dormant volcanoes have not erupted recently, but may erupt in the future.

Active volcanoes have erupted within the last ten thousand years.

Varieties of volcanoes

Volcanoes come in different shapes and sizes.

Caldera
Shaped like a **big bowl**, this volcano is created when the magma chamber collapses.

Cinder cone
This small, steep, **cone-shaped** volcano usually has less powerful eruptions.

Stratovolcano
This large and dangerous volcano is made of **many layers** of lava and ash.

Shield
This wide volcano has **gently sloping** sides, resulting in calmer eruptions.

Italy

Pompeii

Pompeii: a city lost and found

On August 24 nearly 2,000 years ago, people were visiting the marketplace and preparing for lunch in the Roman city of Pompeii in southern Italy. Suddenly, the ground began to shake.

Mount Vesuvius and Pompeii

The nearby volcano, Mount Vesuvius, was erupting. Poisonous gases filled the air, clouds of smoke blocked the sun, and hot ash and rocks rained down on the busy city.

Some people ran to escape, while others hid in their homes. Around 2,000 people lost their lives.

Hidden city

Covered by volcanic ash, Pompeii **disappeared from view** for hundreds of years. It was uncovered in 1748, revealing that ash had helped to preserve the city and its people.

Pompeii's amphitheater

Pompeii had an amphitheater where gladiators did battle, as well as public baths, theaters, and businesses such as bakeries. Bread was found still baking in the ovens.

Molded in plaster

Life-like forms of the volcano's victims were created by pouring plaster into the spaces surrounding skeletons in the ash. These spaces were once filled by the victims' bodies.

Living with volcanoes

Millions of people around the world **live near** volcanoes. This may sound dangerous, but there are reasons why the location **makes perfect sense**.

Asia

North America

Australia

Ring of Fire

The Ring of Fire is an explosive area around the **edges of the Pacific Ocean**. It is home to around three-quarters of the world's **active volcanoes**.

Osorno Volcano and city of Puerto Varas, Chile, South America

Understanding risk

Many volcanoes are **dormant** or even **extinct**, so they are not dangerous. For **active** volcanoes, scientists use tools to monitor levels of activity and predict future eruptions.

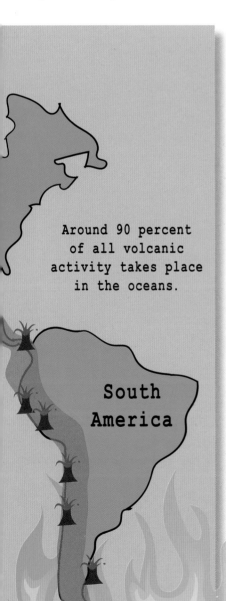

Around 90 percent of all volcanic activity takes place in the oceans.

South America

Hot spots

Here are some **benefits** of living near volcanoes.

Farmland
The **volcanic soil** surrounding volcanoes is **rich** and **fertile**, and this helps farm crops grow.

Tourism
Volcanoes are often a **tourist attraction**. Visitors spend money and support local businesses.

Power
Energy released from volcanoes can be used to produce **electric power** very **cheaply** without harming the environment.

Mineral deposits
Volcanic land contains **useful** and **valuable minerals**, including diamonds, magnesium, and potassium.

Magma beneath

Hot springs are created by magma—**underground rock** that is so **hot** it has become **liquid**. The magma heats **solid rocks** nearby, which then heat any **water** they touch.

Hot spring

Heated water

Hot springs

In some places on Earth, the ground is so hot that it **heats water**. A place where naturally heated water comes up from the ground is known as a hot spring.

Grand Prismatic Spring in Yellowstone

Microbes

Beautiful colors

The colors seen in some hot springs, such as the Grand Prismatic Spring in Yellowstone National Park are caused by **microbes**—tiny living things in the water.

Magma

Sometimes dangerous

The water in hot springs is often so hot that it **boils**. Hot spring water can also be **acidic**, which means it contains a chemical that would hurt our skin if we touched it.

Blue Lagoon spa in Iceland

Safe to swim

Some hot springs are warm rather than hot, and not acidic. These hot springs are safe and fun for us to swim in.

Look, but don't touch! This hot spring is definitely not a good place to swim.

Monkeying around

It's not just humans who have realized how lovely and warm hot springs can be. **Japanese macaques** live in cold, snowy areas of Japan. These monkeys warm up and relax in hot springs!

47

Geysers

Hot springs called geysers shoot jets of **steam** and **superheated water** high up into the sky.

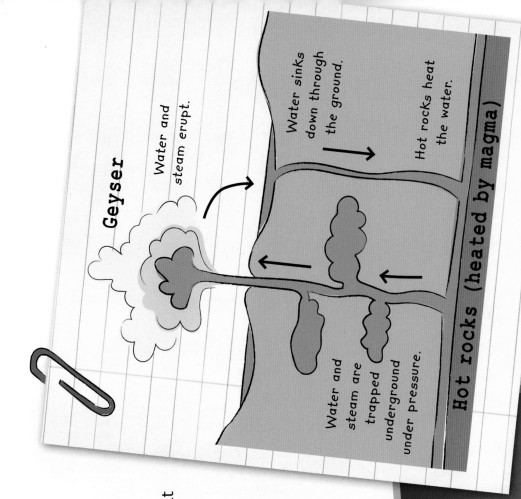

Geyser

Water and steam erupt.

Water sinks down through the ground.

Hot rocks heat the water.

Water and steam are trapped underground under pressure.

Hot rocks (heated by magma)

A geyser at El Tatio, Chile

How it works

Where **hot rocks** and **underground water** meet, the water can heat to boiling point and create **steam**. The trapped underground steam causes **pressure**, which forces the steam and the water above it to erupt.

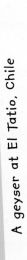

Old Faithful

Located in Yellowstone National Park in Wyoming, Old Faithful is one of the world's **most famous** geysers. It erupts regularly, once every nintey minutes or so.

One...   Two...   Three...   Whoosh!

Old Faithful

There are around 1,000 geysers in the world.

The word "geyser" comes from an Icelandic word "geysir" meaning "to gush."

Saturn

Enceladus

Galactic geysers

There are even geysers in **outer space**! Spacecraft have spotted them, including one on **Enceladus, Saturn's moon.**

Stinky vents

Hold your nose when **hot**, **sulphurous gases** enter the air! These smelly, steamy gases are released through vents near volcanoes, called **fumaroles**.

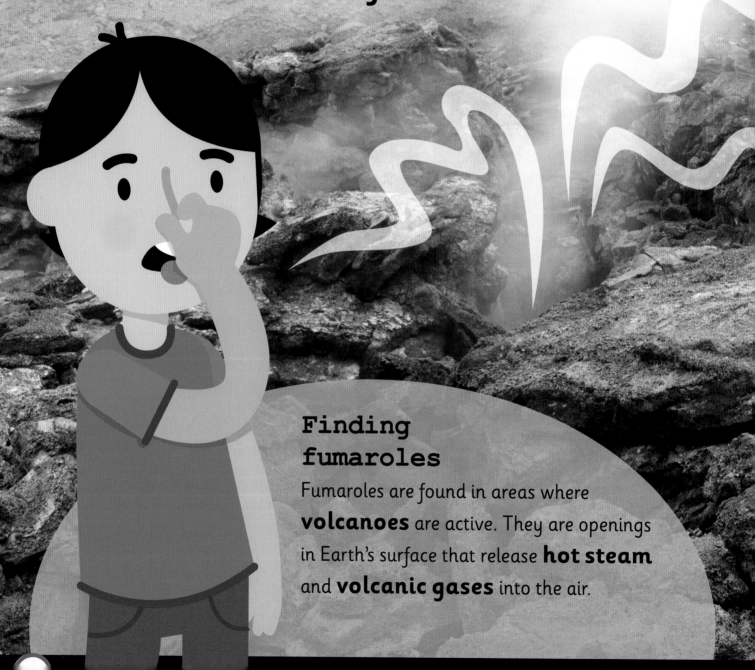

Finding fumaroles

Fumaroles are found in areas where **volcanoes** are active. They are openings in Earth's surface that release **hot steam** and **volcanic gases** into the air.

Kilauea Volcano, Hawaii

The main gases produced by a fumarole are carbon dioxide, sulphur dioxide, and hydrogen sulphide. They are not only seriously smelly, but also dangerous.

Volcano

Water and steam rushes to the surface.

How does it work?

Fumaroles occur on or next to volcanoes when small amounts of water are **boiled** underground. The water turns to **steam**, then travels up and out of vents, along with dangerous volcanic gases.

In freezing cold places such as the Arctic, fumaroles look like magical snow chimneys. This is because the steam freezes and turns to ice, which piles up around the volcanic vent.

often smells like rotten eggs!

Mountains

Majestic mountains create the world's most dramatic skylines. Mountains form over **millions of years** as pieces of Earth's crust smash together and push up into **towering peaks**.

Peak
The highest point of a mountain

Summit
The top area of a mountain

Face
A vertical side of a mountain

Crag
A steep cliff or steep, rocky part of a mountain

The Matterhorn mountain in the Alps, Europe

Making mountains

When two of the **tectonic plates** that make up Earth's surface crash into each other, one of them can get pushed up. **Fold-like** structures are created, making a new mountain range.

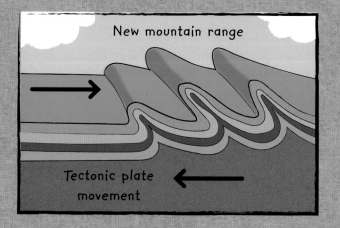

New mountain range

Tectonic plate movement

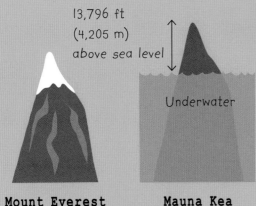

13,796 ft
(4,205 m)
above sea level

Underwater

Mount Everest

Mauna Kea

Mountain peaks

Mount Everest in Nepal is often thought to be the world's tallest mountain. But if mountains were measured from the ocean floor, **Mauna Kea** in Hawaii would be the highest mountain. It is taller than Everest, but only the top part of it is above sea level.

Slope
The side of a mountain

Range
A group of mountains

Pass
Any gap between mountains

On top of the world
Mountains are often cold, snowy, and windy, but life survives here. At least **one billion people** live in the mountains, as well as **many animals**.

Mountain hares have thick fur, which keeps them warm in cold temperatures.

Rocks

Rocks on our planet form over millions of years. There are three main types of rock: **igneous**, **metamorphic**, and **sedimentary**. Each type is created by a different process.

The moon is covered in igneous rock.

Igneous

Igneous rocks such as granite and pumice form when hot, liquid rock **cools down** and hardens. This can happen inside Earth or on its surface.

Granite

Lava (hot, liquid magma rock on Earth's surface) becomes solid igneous rock as it cools.

Pumice

Pumice
Pumice is **full of holes** and can **float** on water! It can be used to remove dead skin from feet. Ugh!

Metamorphic

Metamorphic rocks such as gneiss, marble, and slate are formed from rocks that **undergo change** because of **heat**, **pressure**, or **both**. Hot magma causes the heat. The pressure is caused by tectonic plates meeting.

Gneiss

Marble

Marble is **smooth** and **easy to shape**, so it is often used to make sculptures and buildings. It forms from limestone rock (such as chalk) that has undergone change.

Marble statue

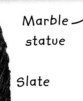
Slate

Sedimentary

Sedimentary rocks such as chalk and coal are made of **sand**, **mud**, and **dead animals and plants**. These things form **layers** that slowly harden into rock.

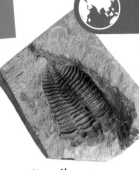

Fossils are formed from the once-living things that hardened into sedimentary rock.

Chalk

Chalk cliffs in Sussex, UK

Coal

Coal is a **fossil fuel**. It can be burned to turn turbines that create **electricity**.

Coal

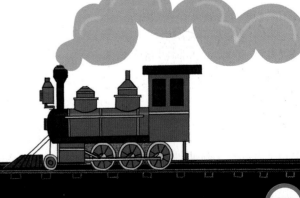
Steam trains often burn coal as fuel.

Rocks on the move

Rocks are not as permanent as they appear. **Action** inside Earth's crust and on its surface keeps rocks **moving** and **changing** in a natural and never-ending cycle.

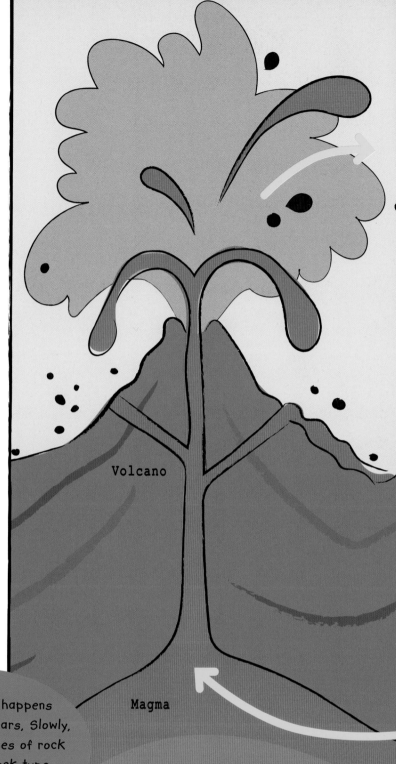

Volcano

Magma

The rock cycle happens over millions of years. Slowly, Earth's three types of rock change—one rock type turns into another.

6 Melted rock

Deep underground, rocks can get heated so much that they melt and turn into liquid rock, called magma. The magma may cool underground and become solid igneous rock.

1 Eruption

Magma (liquid rock) is pushed up to Earth's surface as lava during volcanic eruptions. When this liquid lava rock cools on Earth's surface, it turns into igneous rock.

The rock cycle

The three types of rock—**igneous**, **metamorphic**, and **sedimentary**—are transformed over time by natural processes. The rock cycle sees these three rock types slowly turn into each other.

2 On the move

Rocks on Earth's surface are broken into little pieces by wind and rain. These little pieces of rock, called sediment, are transported by the wind or rain and deposited in oceans and lakes.

3 Piling up

In the oceans and lakes, the sediment piles up, along with dead animals and plants. This all squashes together to form sedimentary rock.

Lake

5 Upthrust

Metamorphic rock and sedimentary rock can be pushed up by movements in Earth's crust, making mountains.

4 Heat and pressure

Heat from under the ground, and pressure from heavy land or water above, turn the sedimentary rock into metamorphic rock.

57

Minerals

Garnet

Turquoise

Rocks are made up of **natural chemicals**, called **minerals**. Some minerals form **sparkling crystals**. Minerals can be put to good use in a variety of wonderful ways.

Green chrysocolla

Topaz

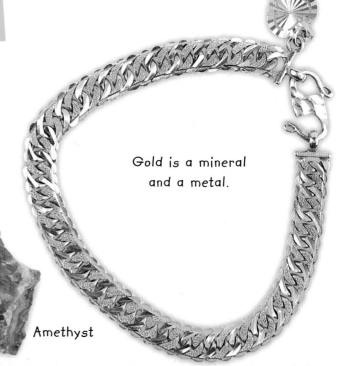
Mica

Minerals come in different colors and textures.

Colossal crystals
The world's **biggest crystals** are in the **Cave of the Crystals** in **Mexico**. These record-breaking crystals are made from a mineral called selenite.

Cave of the Crystals, Mexico

Mineral formation
Minerals formed **inside the Earth many millions of years ago**. Almost all rocks contain at least two minerals.

Gold is a mineral and a metal.

Fire opal

Labradorite

Amethyst

Mineral marvels

Minerals are found all over the world. Here are some of the most **brilliant** and **beautiful** examples.

Calcite

This mineral is found in limestone and marble. It forms stalactites and stalagmites on the ceilings and floors of limestone caves.

Feldspar

Found in granite, feldspar is used in materials such as plastics, ceramics, and glass.

Pyrite

Sparkling and yellow-colored, this mineral can easily be mistaken for gold. It is also known as "fool's gold."

Halite

Known as "rock salt," halite is a type of salt. (Salt comes from seawater, too.) Halite is also used to grit roads in icy winters.

Quartz

In prehistoric times, people used quartz to make sharp flint weapons for hunting. Today, quartz is found in watches, clocks, and electronics.

Gold

Gold has been popular since ancient times. Rare, superstrong, and easy to shape, it is often used in jewelry.

Diamond

Made of carbon, diamond is the hardest natural material on Earth. Glittering diamond gemstones are popular in engagement rings.

Land and sea

From vast blue oceans, icy glaciers, flowing rivers, and peaceful lakes to rocky caves, towering sand dunes, striking craters, and windswept islands, our planet is full of **incredible places**. Let's visit them and find out all about them...

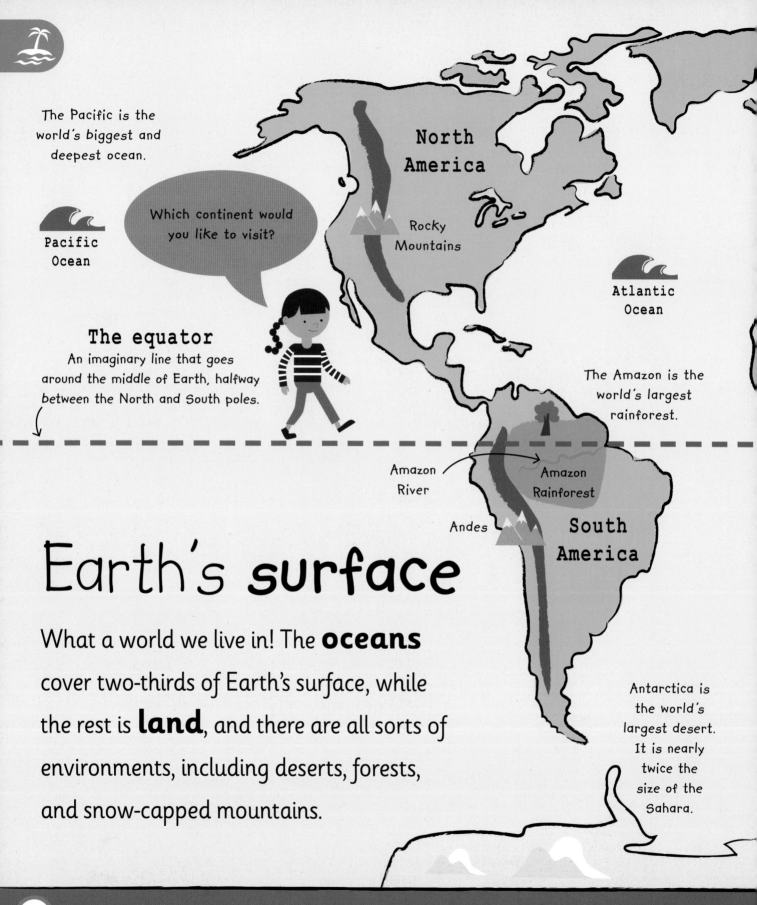

The Pacific is the world's biggest and deepest ocean.

Pacific Ocean

Which continent would you like to visit?

The equator
An imaginary line that goes around the middle of Earth, halfway between the North and South poles.

North America

Rocky Mountains

Atlantic Ocean

The Amazon is the world's largest rainforest.

Amazon River

Amazon Rainforest

Andes

South America

Antarctica is the world's largest desert. It is nearly twice the size of the Sahara.

Earth's surface

What a world we live in! The **oceans** cover two-thirds of Earth's surface, while the rest is **land**, and there are all sorts of environments, including deserts, forests, and snow-capped mountains.

World maps like this show the round Earth

Arctic Ocean

Alps

Europe

Asia is the world's largest continent.

Gobi Desert

Asia

Yangtze River

Himalayas

Pacific Ocean

Atlas Mountains

Nile River

Mount Everest is the world's tallest mountain above sea level.

Sahara Desert

Southeast Asian Rainforest

Congo Rainforest

Indian Ocean

Africa

Physical map

There are many different types of maps. This physical map includes the **landscapes** of our world. It uses colors and symbols to show different landscapes, such as mountains and rainforests.

Great Sandy Desert

Australasia

Southern Ocean

Antarctica

on a flat surface.

Even mega-sized mountains can eventually be worn away!

Wearing away

Weather, **waves**, **rivers**, and **living things** can break down Earth's rocks, wearing them away. Over millions of years, huge rocks can be shaped and changed.

Rainwater can cause chemical weathering, breaking up rock.

Weathering or erosion?

When rock is **changed** or **broken apart** but **stays where it is**, this is called weathering. When rock is **broken down** then **carried away**, this is called erosion.

Pieces of rock are carried away, eroded by rain.

We're busy digging our burrow.

Weathering or erosion can be caused by animals breaking up rock.

Forces of nature

Weather and **water** both play their part in erosion, wearing down rocks and carrying away the tiny broken pieces.

Water erosion
Water from rain and winding rivers can carve out valleys and steep gorges. The Grand Canyon has been carved by the Colorado River.

Wind erosion
Wind can transform rock, especially in deserts. Sand carried by the wind rubs against exposed rock, wearing it away. Over thousands of years, wind and sand have carved striking rock formations in the White Desert, in Egypt.

Coastal erosion
Coastlines are affected by waves hitting rocky cliffs. Rock breaks away from the cliffs, leaving behind caves and arches. The Twelve Apostles in Australia are large limestone stacks caused by coastal erosion.

Plant roots can cause weathering, cracking rock.

A river can erode pieces of rock, washing them away.

Wind shapes

The **power** of the wind works wonders on the world's landscapes. It carries sand and dust and **wears away** surfaces, transforming rocks into unique shapes.

Rock pedestal

Also known as **mushroom rocks**, these **top-heavy structures** form as the wind wears away softer rock near the ground.

Mushroom Rock
State Park in Kansas

Yardang

High ridges alongside **deep troughs** are called yardangs. They form when the wind wears away looser rock. The ridges and troughs lie in the same direction as the wind blows.

Hoodoo

Better known as **fairy chimneys**, hoodoos are **tall rocks** with **basalt heads** on top. Without the tough basalt heads to protect them from the wind, hoodoos would break down and eventually disappear.

The tough basalt top protects the softer rock below.

In Turkey, people have carved out houses in hoodoos.

Hoodoos in Cappadocia, Turkey

Dunhuang Yardang National Geopark in China

Uluru, an inselberg in Australia

Inselberg

An inselberg **rises on its own** from **flat ground**. The wind has eroded the rock around the inselberg more quickly, leaving behind the small mountain.

Sand dunes

Desert landscapes change because of the **wind**. As gusts blow, billions of sand grains are shaped into sand dunes.

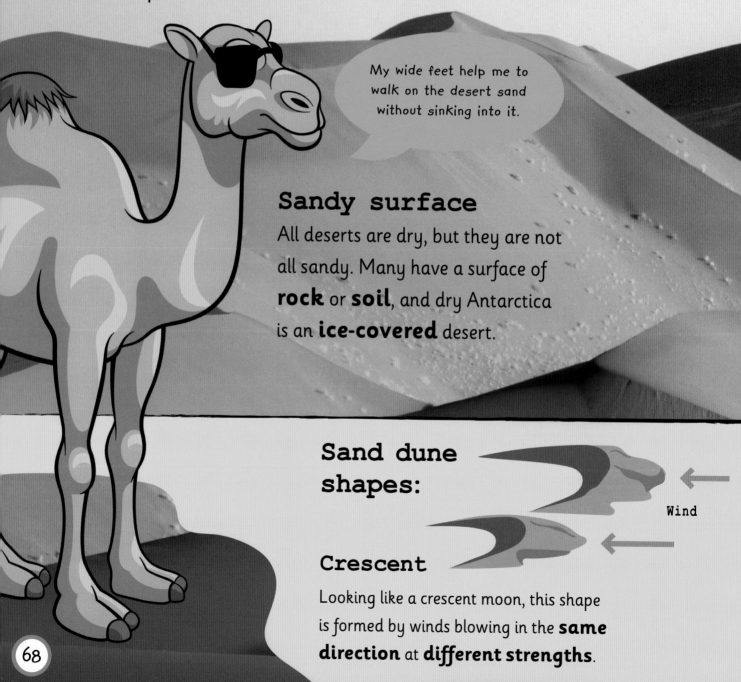

My wide feet help me to walk on the desert sand without sinking into it.

Sandy surface

All deserts are dry, but they are not all sandy. Many have a surface of **rock** or **soil**, and dry Antarctica is an **ice-covered** desert.

Sand dune shapes:

Wind

Crescent

Looking like a crescent moon, this shape is formed by winds blowing in the **same direction** at **different strengths**.

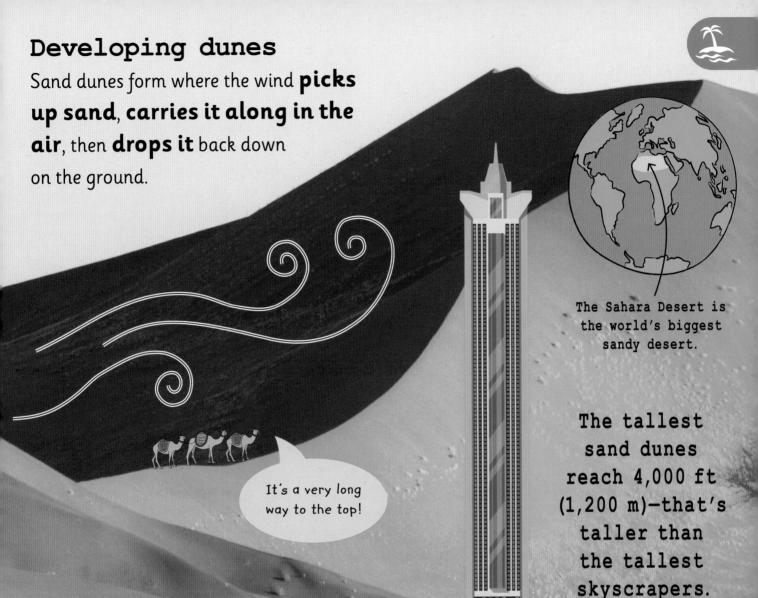

Developing dunes

Sand dunes form where the wind **picks up sand**, **carries it along in the air**, then **drops it** back down on the ground.

The Sahara Desert is the world's biggest sandy desert.

It's a very long way to the top!

The tallest sand dunes reach 4,000 ft (1,200 m)—that's taller than the tallest skyscrapers.

Transverse

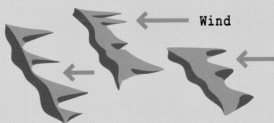

Wind

Transverse dunes are long with wavy ridges. They are made by winds blowing **a lot of sand** in **one direction**.

Star

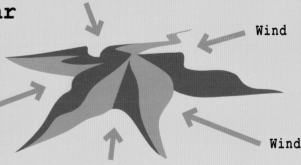

Wind

Wind

Among the tallest sand dunes, star dunes form when the wind blows in **all directions**.

Impact craters
Meteorites are **rocks** from **outer space** that **crash** into Planet Earth. Large meteorites can create impact craters when they hit the ground.

Impact craters can be seen on moons and other planets in the solar system.

Craters

BOOM! Meteorites and erupting volcanoes create striking marks on Earth's surface. They make bowl-shaped **dents**, called craters. Craters can also be made by explosions that are caused by human activities.

Hidden craters
There are around **175 impact craters** on Earth. But most of them can **no longer be seen** because they have been worn away by rain and wind, or covered by layers of rock and soil.

Meteor Crater in Arizona is a meteorite crater.

Around 3,000 meteorites hit Earth every year, but very few are big enough to make craters.

Mount Bromo volcano crater in East Java, Indonesia

Chicxulub Crater

Chicxulub Crater in Mexico is an impact crater that is now buried. It was caused by a meteorite 65 million years ago. The resulting devastation is thought to have **wiped out the dinosaurs**, along with many other **plants** and **animals**.

Volcano craters

Hot rock and lava explode out of active volcanoes. These **outward explosions** create huge volcano craters. Most volcano craters are **summit craters**, found at the very tops of volcanoes.

Soil

The soil covering our world is **essential to life on Earth**. It is home to everything from roots and rotting plants to worms and woodlice. Grab a spade and get digging!

The topsoil is where 95 percent of the world's food is grown.

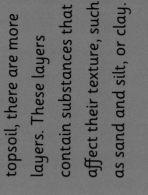

Soil layers

There are **many layers of soil,** starting with the humus layer, and then the topsoil layer. Under the topsoil, there are more layers. These layers contain substances that affect their texture, such as sand and silt, or clay.

The **humus layer** is made of dead, rotting plants and animals.

The **topsoil** is full of lively creatures and food for plants.

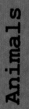

Animals

All kinds of creatures **set up their homes** in the soil. There's water here for them to **drink**, as well as rotting plants to **feed on**, while the darkness of the soil keeps them **safe** and **protected** from animals that would eat them.

The **leaching layer** is mostly sand and silt.

The **subsoil layer** contains clay and minerals from underground rock.

The **weathered rock layer**, or **regolith**, contains rocks that have broken off from the solid bedrock below.

Plants

Trees and other plants use soil as a solid base so that they can stand upright. Plant roots spread down into the soil like anchors. The roots also take in water and food from the soil.

What's in soil?

Soil may look dark and dull, but it is **packed** with pieces of rock, useful nutrients, crawling creatures, rotten plants, dead animals, gases, and water. **Wow!**

Soil gives the gift of life

Without soil, plants cannot grow, and Earth's plants give out oxygen, and are food for many animals. Some animals also live in soil, or eat animals that live there.

Bedrock

Water

Nothing can live without water. Humans, all other animals, and plants need water to stay **alive** and **healthy**.

Many uses

Think of how many times you use water. As well as **drinking it**, you use it to **bathe**, **clean**, and **prepare dinner**. And don't forget we can **swim** in it, too! **Splash!**

Mostly saltwater

There is more water on the surface of Earth than any other substance, and **97.5 percent** of it is saltwater, found in the oceans. Saltwater contains sodium chloride, commonly known as **salt**. We can't drink it.

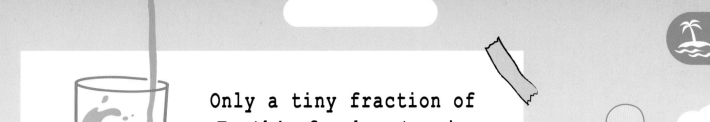

Only a tiny fraction of Earth's fresh water is in lakes and rivers and easily accessible as drinking water.

Around two-thirds of your whole body is water!

Fresh water

Only **2.5 percent** of Earth's water is fresh water that **doesn't contain salt**. Most of this is trapped in **ice**, a tiny amount is **water vapor** in the air, and around a third of it is in the **ground**. This groundwater seeps into lakes and rivers, and can be treated to make drinking water.

Amount of fresh water in the air

Amount of fresh water in the ground

Amount of fresh water that is frozen in ice caps and glaciers

Rivers

Flowing rivers are a **beautiful sight**, but where do they come from and where do they go?

Go with the flow

Rivers are **different lengths**, and can be **slow or fast moving**. They usually **run downhill**.

The source of a river is the place where it starts.

Tributaries are streams that flow into the main river.

Steep, V-shaped valleys are created by rushing water wearing away surrounding rock.

From start to finish

A river usually starts in the **hills** or **mountains**. Rain falls, and the water comes together in little streams. The streams join up, making a river that runs across the land, usually ending **in the ocean**.

River courses

The **upper course** of a river is where the water flows fastest. Here there are waterfalls and steep valleys. The **middle course** of a river has big sweeping bends. The **lower course** is where the water slows down and empties out into the ocean.

The place where a large river meets the ocean is called an estuary.

The river leaves mud and sand behind on the floodplain.

Riverbanks are the sides of the river.

Meanders are winding bends along the river.

A floodplain is an area of flat, fertile land beside a river that gets covered in water if the river floods.

The Amazon River in South America is the widest river in the world and has the largest amount of water. Amazing animals such as river dolphins and anacondas live here, as well as around two thousand types of fish, including electric eels.

77

Ledge of
hard rock

Waterfalls

Breathtaking waterfalls show us the **incredible power** of nature.

Soft
rock

Waterfall creation

Waterfalls are created where the rock under a river changes from **hard rock** to **soft rock**. The force of the water **wears away** the soft rock. This leaves a **ledge** of hard rock, with rushing water flowing over it.

Niagara Falls

Magnificent Niagara

Every second, an amount of water that could fill up an **Olympic-size swimming pool** flows over the cliffs at Niagara Falls, on the border between the United States and Canada.

Waterfall daredevil

In 1853, Frenchman Charles Blondin crossed Niagara Falls, walking along a tightrope without any safety equipment!

Blondin repeated the stunt around three hundred times. He did it in many ways, including backward, with someone on his back, on stilts, and blindfolded!

Charles Blondin

River rapids

Areas of **swirling white water**, called rapids, are often near waterfalls. In these areas, soft rock has been worn down, leaving hard rocks standing up in the water. The river swirls around the hard rocks.

Hard rock

Soft rock

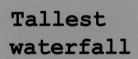

Angel Falls

Tallest waterfall

In 1933, American pilot Jimmy Angel was flying over Venezuela when he spotted a waterfall that turned out to be the world's tallest. It was named **Angel Falls** after him.

Adult kayakers like me train for a long time to be able to race over rapids.

79

Glaciers

Glaciers are **gigantic masses** of **snow** and **ice** that build up over hundreds of years, and **move slowly** over the land. Visiting one is like going to an extreme winter wonderland!

Glacier formation

Most glaciers develop high in the mountains. **Fallen snow piles up** and **presses together**. This creates a solid block of snow and ice that flows slowly downhill.

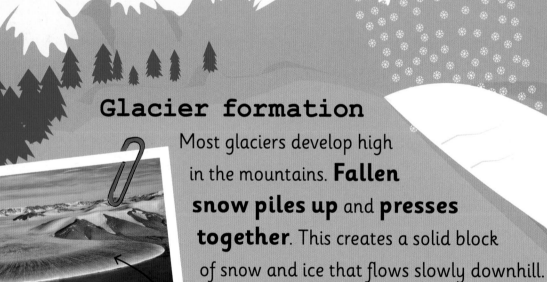

Accumulation zones are places where the deepest snow piles up over time.

Elephant Foot Glacier

A stream or lake forms as parts of the glacier melt.

The Elephant Foot Glacier in Greenland is the same shape as an elephant's foot!

Around 10 percent of Earth's land is covered with glacial ice.

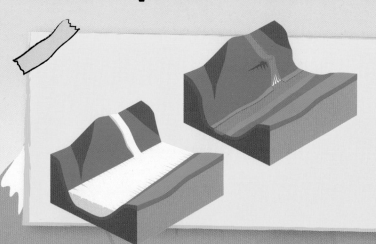

After a glacier
As glaciers move, they pick up rocks and grit. This rough material wears away at the land under the moving glacier, carving out deep, U-shaped valleys. Streams and rivers often flow where glaciers once were.

Snail speed
Glaciers may look like they aren't moving, but they are actually **creeping steadily** downhill, pulled along by their own weight.

Even I move faster than a glacier!

Terminal moraines are ridges of rock and soil that are left behind at the front of the glacier when it melts.

Glacier terminus

Glacier terminus
The point **where a glacier ends** is called the glacier terminus, or snout. Some glaciers stop farther down a mountain where it gets warmer. Others continue to the coast and become **floating ice shelves** in the sea.

Caves

Caves are **dark**, **damp**, and **mysterious** places. They're perfect for exploring—what are you waiting for?

> My cave home protects me from bad weather.

Cave creatures

Many animals set up home in the safe shelter of caves. For example, **bears** snuggle down and sleep through the winter in caves, and **bats** rest in them during the daytime.

Some types of caves

Rocky caves

Most caves form when **rainwater wears away** limestone, marble, or gypsum rock.

Lava caves

A **lava flow** (liquid rock from an erupting volcano) can cool and harden at the edges, forming a **lava tube**. When the volcano stops erupting, flowing lava pours out of the tube, leaving a tunnel-like cave.

What are caves?

Caves are **large**, **natural hollows** in the ground, a hillside, or a cliff face. They are big enough for you to fit in!

Caves often form when rainwater wears away rocks, such as limestone.

2

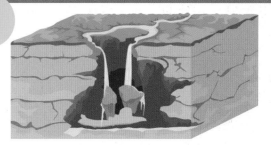

Over time, weaker parts of the rock are worn away by the rainwater.

1

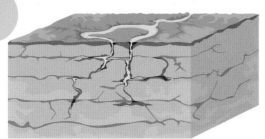

Rainwater falls through cracks in the limestone rock.

3

Eventually, caves are created.

Ice caves

When **ice melts** on a **glacier's surface**, the water flows down into the glacier, slowly **carving out** ice caves.

Coastal caves

When **waves** crash against the coast, **cracks** develop in **cliffs**. The waves continue to **wear away** the rock, forming caves.

Columns of **rock**

Rock formations inside caves come in all sorts of shapes. Some **stand up** on the floor, while others **hang down** from the ceiling.

Stalactites

Water dripping through the cave ceiling carries pieces of limestone. Some limestone is left behind by the water, creating **dangling shapes**, called stalactites. They get steadily longer.

Stalagmites

Water dripping onto the cave floor mixes with rocky limestone to create pillars of rock **rising up from the ground**, called stalagmites. They get taller over time.

REMEMBER:
Stalactites hang tight!
Stalagmites rise up
from the ground.

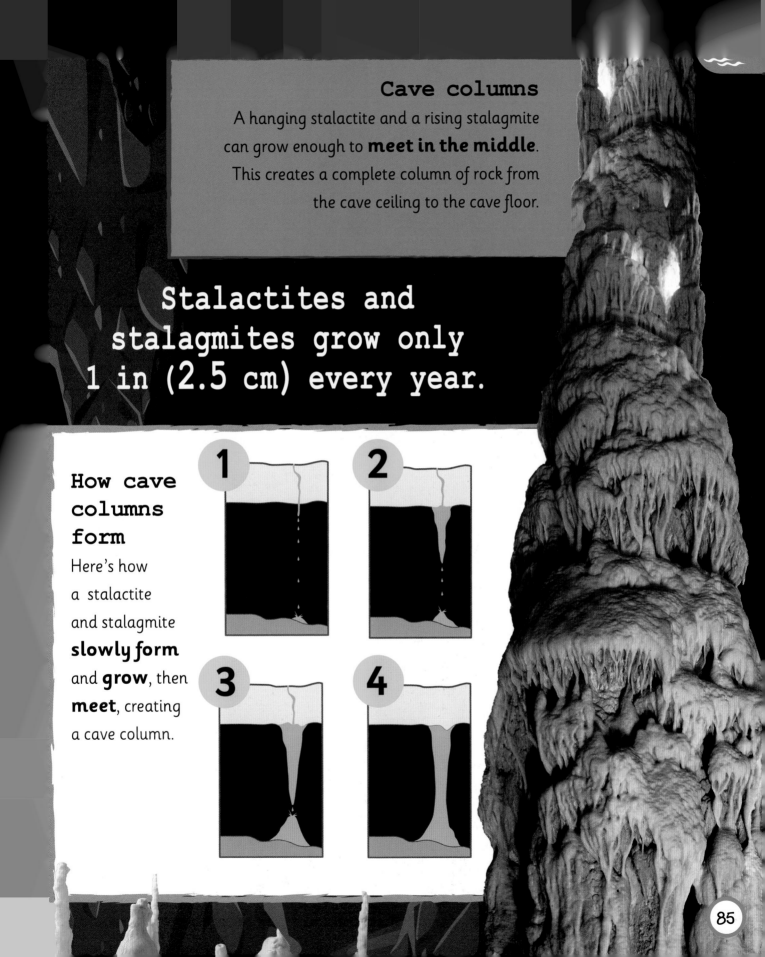

Cave columns

A hanging stalactite and a rising stalagmite can grow enough to **meet in the middle**. This creates a complete column of rock from the cave ceiling to the cave floor.

Stalactites and stalagmites grow only 1 in (2.5 cm) every year.

How cave columns form

Here's how a stalactite and stalagmite **slowly form** and **grow**, then **meet**, creating a cave column.

1

2

3

4

Lakes

Imagine the biggest puddle on a rainy day. This is basically a very small lake! Lakes are **expanses** of **fresh water** or occasionally **saltwater** that are surrounded by land.

> I love windsurfing on a lake!

Make a lake

Lakes develop over hundreds or thousands of years in **hollows** caused by sunken earth, icy glaciers, or erupting volcanoes. The hollows **fill with water**, becoming lakes.

Open or closed?

If water moves out of a lake into a river or stream, the lake is said to be an **open lake**. If water doesn't move out of a lake, the lake is said to be **closed**.

> Most closed lakes have salty water. The salt comes from salty minerals in the lake water.

Oxbow lake

These **horseshoe-shaped** lakes form from a bend in a river.

1

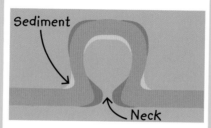

A river flows over the land, winding along in bends called meanders.

2

The river drops off sediment (small pieces of rock).

Sediment

Neck

The neck of the meander gets narrower.

3

The river cuts across the narrow neck—the shortest part of the meander loop.

Oxbow lake

A separate horseshoe-shaped oxbow lake is left behind.

Lake Baikal

Old and deep

The world's oldest and deepest lake is **Lake Baikal** in Siberia, Russia. It is twenty-five million years old and holds around 20 percent of Earth's unfrozen fresh water!

There are around 117 million lakes on Earth.

The Dead Sea

Despite its name, the Dead Sea is a **saltwater lake**. Located on the border between Israel and Jordan, this lake's water is **nine times saltier** than seawater. It is so full of salt that it is denser (thicker) than the human body, so people float in the Dead Sea.

Floating in the Dead Sea

Oceans and seas

More than two-thirds of Earth's surface is oceans and seas. No wonder it is called the **blue planet!**

Dive in!

Oceans are **gigantic pools of saltwater**. They formed four billion years ago, when water filled up hollows on Earth. There are **five oceans**— the Pacific, Atlantic, Indian, Southern, and Arctic, and more than **fifty seas**.

Chukchi Sea

Beaufort Sea

Baffin Bay

Bering Sea

Hudson Bay

Labrador Sea

Sargasso Sea

Atlantic Ocean

Caribbean Sea

Pacific Ocean

Scotia Sea

Ocean or sea?
Oceans are **very large expanses** of water. They are **much bigger** than seas. Seas form **part** of an **ocean** or are **partly enclosed by land**.

The five oceans:

Pacific Ocean
This is the biggest ocean. It contains more water than all the other oceans and seas put together!

Atlantic Ocean
The Atlantic Ocean is the second-biggest ocean. It is the saltiest ocean because water evaporates the most here.

Amazing oceans

Our oceans are something to celebrate! More than **225,000 types of marine life** live in them, around two-thirds of the world's **oxygen supply** comes from ocean plants, and ocean waters give us **seafood**.

Map labels

Greenland Sea

Arctic Ocean

Laplev Sea

East Siberian Sea

Barents Sea

Norwegian Sea

Kara Sea

White Sea

Sea of Okhotsk

Baltic Sea

Black Sea

North Sea

Yellow Sea

Sea of Japan (East Sea)

Mediterranean Sea

Bay of Biscay

Pacific Ocean

East China Sea

Arabian Sea

Red Sea

Bay of Bengal

South China Sea

Philippine Sea

Golf of Aden

Andaman Sea

Celebes Sea

Flores Sea

Arafuna Sea

Java Sea

Timor Sea

Coral Sea

Indian Ocean

Tasman Sea

Southern Ocean

Sea or lake?

To be a sea, a body of water must be **connected to an ocean**. Earth's biggest lakes are larger than its smallest seas!

Indian Ocean
The third-biggest ocean is the Indian Ocean. It is the warmest ocean.

Southern Ocean
The fourth-biggest ocean is the Southern Ocean. Its icy water surrounds Antarctica.

Arctic Ocean
The Arctic Ocean is the smallest, shallowest, and coldest ocean.

Jacques Cousteau
and the Blue Hole

The Great Blue Hole in the Caribbean Sea remained a mystery until French explorer **Jacques Cousteau** visited it in 1971. This **giant hole** in the ocean floor is so big that it can be seen from outer space.

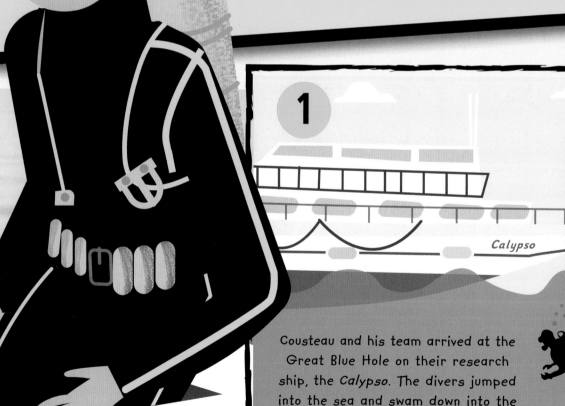

1

Calypso

Cousteau and his team arrived at the Great Blue Hole on their research ship, the *Calypso*. The divers jumped into the sea and swam down into the darkness of the giant hole.

2

There were sharks in the water and a sucker fish tried to nibble one diver's legs! The team was amazed by the size of the hole. It was enormous and far too deep for them to reach the very bottom.

3

The divers found stalagmites and stalactites. These rocky shapes develop in air, so the team realized that the hole was once a cave above sea level. Over time, as sea levels rose, the cave's roof collapsed and it filled with water.

4

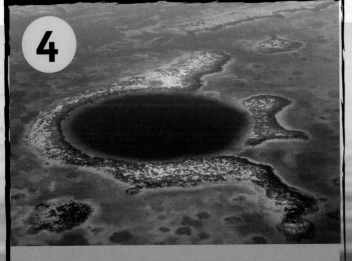

A TV program showed Cousteau's visit, and as a result of his expedition, the Great Blue Hole is now legally protected as a World Heritage Site. It's the largest sinkhole (hole in the ground) in the world!

In 2018, two piloted submarines made it right to the bottom of the Great Blue Hole. The vast limestone floor looked like the surface of the moon and there was no marine life at all.

Islands

When you think of an island, you might imagine one with a beautiful sandy beach. But islands can have **all sorts of landscapes**.

The world's largest island is Greenland, in the Atlantic Ocean. Its surface is mostly covered by glaciers.

Barrier islands

Barrier islands form when **sand piles up between the sea and shore**. These islands change shape due to waves and winds moving the sand around.

Coral islands

Coral islands develop in **tropical waters** from the **piled up skeletons** of **tiny animals** called coral polyps.

Oceanic islands

Oceanic islands develop from **erupting volcanoes on the seabed**. The lava cools and hardens over time, making the volcano taller and taller until it reaches the surface of the sea and becomes an island.

Lava flows from volcanic eruptions are still frequent on the oceanic islands of Hawaii.

Mu Ko Ang Thong National Park is a chain of islands in the Gulf of Thailand.

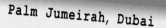

Palm Jumeirah, Dubai

Tidal islands

A tidal island is **attached to the mainland**, but the linking land can only be seen when the tide goes out. At high tide, the linking land is underwater.

Artificial islands

These islands have been **deliberately created by people**. Sand can be dug up and moved to create islands, such as the Palm Jumeirah in Dubai.

Waves

The **motion** of the ocean is wonderful to watch, but **making waves** is a whole other story…

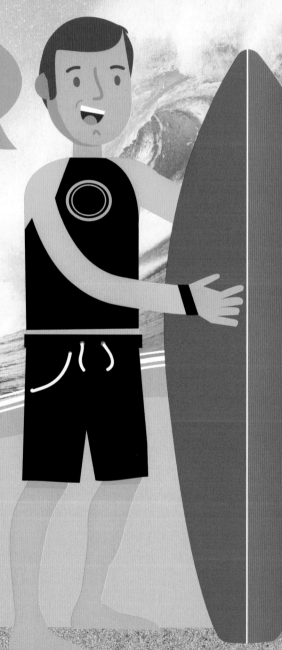

Hi, I'm Garrett McNamara from the United States. In 2013, I surfed a wave that was taller than a ten-story building!

Surfer on a giant wave in Nazaré, Portugal

Wind and waves

The wind produces ocean waves as it blows across the water. Wave size and shape depend on the **wind distance**, **direction**, and **strength**.

Surfers, windsurfers, and kayakers

Ripples

How waves form

Gentle winds cause **little ripples**. If stronger winds blow, **choppy waves** develop. If stronger winds keep blowing, the choppy waves gradually turn into a regular series of large waves rolling across the sea, called **swell**.

Swell

Wave energy

Waves are **energy** passing through the ocean. A wave can make water at the surface **appear to be moving forward** when it **actually isn't**.

Crest of the wave

Trough of the wave

The water isn't moving forward—it is just going **up** and **down** in the **same place**.

As a wave passes **under** an object on the surface, **the object is lifted up**.

After the wave passes, **the object drops** to where it was before.

all use waves for fun!

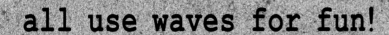

Tides

Tides are the **rising** and **falling** of sea levels. Incredibly, **forces** created by the **moon** are the primary cause of the high and low tides.

Forces at work

As the moon travels around Earth, it creates forces. It **pulls** at the water on one side of our planet, and causes water to **bulge out** on the opposite side. As Earth spins, its coasts pass through these two bulges, creating a daily **rise** and **fall** of water—**our tides**.

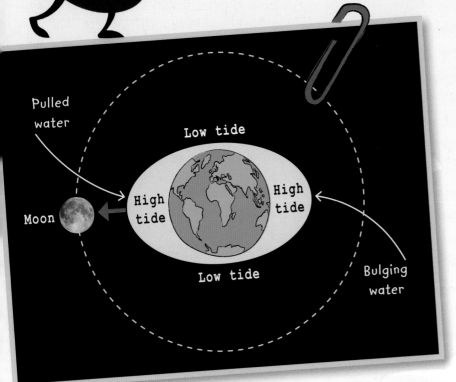

Pulled water

Low tide

High tide

Moon

High tide

Low tide

Bulging water

Carried by the tide

Tides **carry things** onto the shore, including seashells, seaweed, and starfish. You might even find pirate treasure or a message in a bottle!

High tide

When water is at its **highest point** on the beach and there is **more sea than sand**, it is high tide.

Low tide

When water is at its **lowest point** on the beach and there is **more sand than sea**, it is low tide. Most places have two high tides and two low tides each day because our planet spins and different sides of it face the moon.

Weather

The **sun**, the **air**, and **water** on our planet create a range of weather systems. Depending on where you are, you may experience sunshine, rain, thunderstorms, snow, or a mix of them all! There's also extreme weather, such as tornadoes and hurricanes.

What is weather?

Weather happens all around us all the time. Sometimes the **sun** has its hat on, but at other times, **raindrops** keep falling on your head!

Weather workings

Weather is caused by the **sun**, the **air**, and **water**. The sun produces heat, air moves to make wind, and water creates rain and snow.

All sorts of weather

The weather can be **sunny**, **cloudy**, **windy**, **rainy**, or **snowy**.

Sunny

The sun warms up the air, resulting in hot temperatures.

Cloudy

Water vapor (very tiny drops of water in the air that you can't see) rises from the ground. The vapor cools and becomes liquid water droplets that build into clouds.

Weather takes place in the atmosphere,

The highest temperature ever recorded was 134°F (56°C), measured in 1913 in Death Valley, California.

Weather forecast

Weather forecasts **try to predict** what the weather will be. Checking the forecast can help you plan what to do and what to wear.

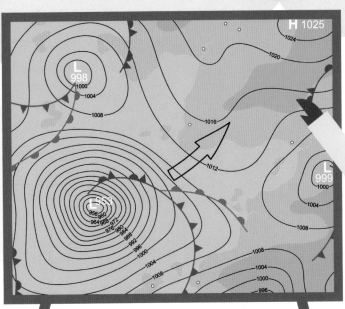

A weather forecast

The coldest temperature ever recorded was -128°F (-89°C), measured in 1983 at Russia's Vostok research station in Antarctica.

Windy	Rainy	Snowy
Windy days happen when air moves around quickly.	Rain falls when the water droplets inside clouds become big and heavy.	Cold temperatures turn water droplets into icy snowflakes.

a layer of gases surrounding our planet.

The water cycle

The water on our planet moves between the land, the sky, and the seas, rivers, and lakes in a **constant looping cycle**.

Nearly all of Earth's water is saltwater in the oceans. Only a tiny fraction is fresh water that we can use as drinking water.

How the cycle works

The **amount** of water on our planet **never changes**. It **travels** to and from different places in an endless cycle.

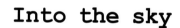

Into the sky

The warmed water becomes **water vapor** (very tiny drops of water in the air that you can't see). This vapor rises up.

Warming up

The **sun's heat** warms water in oceans, lakes, and rivers.

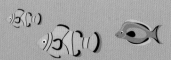

Cooling down

The **cool sky** turns all the water vapor back into **liquid water droplets**.

Clouds

The liquid water droplets build up, making **clouds**.

Falling

The droplets group together and become **heavy**. They fall to Earth as **rain**, **snow**, or **hail**.

Plants also release water vapor into the sky.

Flowing

The water from the rain, snow, or hail flows into **rivers**, **lakes**, and **seas**.

Water is always on the move in the cycle!

How clouds form

Look up at the sky and you may see clouds floating by! Fluffy clouds are made from **tiny droplets of water** hanging in the air.

Sun heats water

When water is heated by the sun, it **evaporates**—it becomes **water vapor** (very tiny drops of water in the air that you can't see).

Creating clouds

When the water vapor meets colder air, it cools and changes into **liquid water droplets**. The droplets group together, making clouds.

The average cloud weighs around the same as two passenger aircraft!

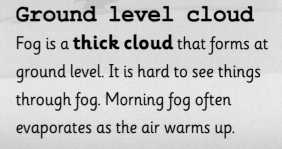

If water vapor changes back into liquid on the ground, it creates sparkling drops of dew.

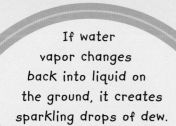

Ground level cloud

Fog is a **thick cloud** that forms at ground level. It is hard to see things through fog. Morning fog often evaporates as the air warms up.

Cloud types

Can you see any clouds today? Are they big and fluffy or wispy and small? Did you know that all clouds can be grouped, based on their **size** and **shape?**

Cirrus
These **wispy clouds** trail across blue skies on sunny days.

Altocumulus
These clouds form in **cool temperatures**, before thunderstorms develop.

Cirrocumulus
These clouds form when **cirrostratus clouds break up** into little pieces.

Cirrostratus
Long and **thin**, these clouds are made from tiny ice crystals.

Altostratus
These **large, thin sheets** of **gray clouds** form when thunderstorms are building.

Why are there different clouds?

The way clouds form depends on their **height** in the sky, the surrounding **temperature**, and the **power** of the **wind**.

Stratus

These **white** or **gray clouds** form **sheets** or **layers** and often cover a lot of the sky.

Nimbostratus

These **flat, dark rain clouds** bring heavy rain or snow.

Cumulonimbus

These **ginormous, tall thunderclouds** produce storms, hurricanes, and tornadoes.

Stratocumulus

These clouds develop in **calm conditions**, or in **gentle rain**, or **light snow**.

Cumulus

These **fluffy, cotton-ball clouds** form on bright, sunny days.

Falling from the sky

Moisture falling from the sky is called **precipitation**. This can be all kinds of wet weather, including **rain**, **hail**, and **snow**.

Hail

Hailstones are **balls** or **pieces of ice**. They form in the cold, top part of storm clouds when water droplets freeze together. More water freezes to the ice pieces, and eventually they fall as hail.

Hail can be as big as tennis balls!

No two snowflakes are ever the same.

Snow

At temperatures below freezing, water vapor in the clouds turns straight into **ice crystals**, which fall as **snowflakes**.

Rain

Rain starts to form when water vapor in the sky cools and changes back into **liquid water droplets**. These water droplets build up, forming clouds. The droplets group together, becoming heavy. They then fall as rain.

These raindrops have come all the way down from the clouds!

Record breakers:

Driest

The driest hot desert on Earth is the Atacama Desert in Chile. Parts of it have had no rain for more than 400 years. Antarctica is Earth's driest cold desert. (Deserts can be hot or cold, but they are always dry.)

Wettest

Mawsynram, in northeast India, is the world's wettest place. Its average rainfall is 467 in (1,187 cm) per year—the same height as two giraffes!

Snowiest

The most snowfall ever recorded was in the Mount Baker Ski Area in Washington, during the winter of 1998 to 1999. There was nearly 98 ft (30 m) of snow—that's the height of a ten-story building!

109

The **Rain Dragon**

Thousands of years ago, before science explained the world's weather, people in **ancient China** thought that rain falling from the sky came from a **winged dragon** called **Yinglong**.

Yinglong, the Rain Dragon

The legend of Yinglong

Yinglong lived in the center of the sky and had **control of the rain**. She was more important than other legendary creatures because she was the water bearer, who **brought life** to the world.

Yinglong's sweat fell as **raindrops** and her fiery breath made **swirling clouds**. Her swishing tail carved out **winding riverbeds** where water could flow.

People called on Yinglong for just the **right amount of rain** to keep **plants** and **crops growing**. They worried about what might happen if she **held back** the rain and caused a **drought**.

They lived in fear of Yinglong **getting angry** and sending **too much rain**, creating **floods**. Legend said that Yinglong had helped two kings by sending floods to destroy lands belonging to their enemies.

People worshipped Yinglong because her water was essential to their survival.

Cloth dragon model

Celebrations today
Today, Yinglong is still remembered at **New Year celebrations** and **rain ceremonies**. Colorful cloth dragons, dances, and parades are all part of the festivities.

Snowstorms and blizzards

Snow covers the landscape in a **sparkling white blanket**. But when there are howling winds, heavy snowfalls, and freezing temperatures, conditions can become dangerous.

Heavy snowfall can leave people stuck inside vehicles or buildings, waiting for the emergency rescue services.

Snowy weather

Snow falls when the temperature in the clouds is **below freezing** and the water vapor in the clouds **turns into ice**. Here are some different types of snowy weather. **Brrrr!**

Snowstorms

In winter, when temperatures drop, **heavy snow** can fall for hours. These snowstorms cause **drifting snow** that buries buildings and blocks roads.

Antarctica

The frozen continent of Antarctica is the **coldest** and **windiest** place on Earth. No one lives here all the time, but scientists visit to work at research stations.

Penguins huddle to keep warm in Antarctica's freezing, windy weather.

Wind speeds in Antarctica can reach 125 miles per hour (200 km per hour)—around twice as fast as a car travels on a highway.

Blizzards

The difference between a snowstorm and a blizzard is not the level of snow, but the **power of the wind**. During blizzards, strong winds blow snow and ice around, making it difficult to see.

Ice storms

Ice storms are rare events, occurring when **rain meets very cold air** near the ground. They cover the landscape in a **layer of ice**.

Thunderstorms

Take cover! Every day there are around **45,000** thunderstorms and **eight million** lightning strikes around the world.

Storms happen more often in hot, humid places.

Stormy weather

Storms put on a spectacular show. The **dark clouds** contain **so much water** that sunlight can't get through. Heavy rain fills the skies, and there are strong winds, lightning flashes, and thunderclaps.

How do storms form?

Heated by the sun, Earth's water turns into water vapor (wet air). The vapor rises, then cools, forming clouds full of water droplets. When there are **big amounts of warm, rising vapor**, massive thunderclouds are created that release very heavy rain.

Warm water vapor rises, then cools and becomes liquid water droplets, forming clouds.

Lightning

A bolt of lightning is a **huge spark of electricity** from a storm cloud. It happens when water droplets and ice crystals bump together inside the cloud, creating an **electric charge**. The electric charge builds up, until lightning is released in a dramatic flash.

Lightning can reach sizzling temperatures more than five times hotter than the surface of the sun.

Thunder

Thunder is the **sound caused by a lightning flash**. The flash of lightning is seen before the crash of thunder is heard because light moves much faster than sound.

CRACK! BOOM!

A lot of warm, wet air rises.

A rainstorm occurs.

The water droplets build up and rise higher and higher, forming tall storm clouds.

The storm will end soon.

When less warm air rises, the clouds start to break up. The storm begins to end.

Monsoons

Every year, tropical countries in southern Asia experience **powerful seasonal winds** and **heavy rainfalls**, called monsoons. This stormy weather causes widespread flooding.

Wind of change

The strong monsoon wind blows in **one direction** during the **summer months** and the **opposite direction** during the **winter months**. The change in direction is caused by differences in land and ocean temperatures.

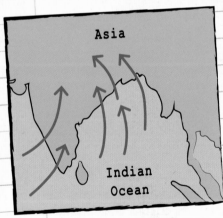

Wet season
Summer winds carry heavy rain to land in monsoon areas, starting the wet season.

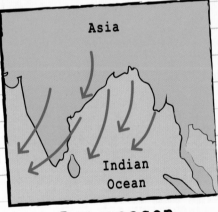

Dry season
Winter winds start the dry season as cold, dry air is blown from the land back to the ocean.

Monsoon rains are the only source of water for two-thirds of the plants grown as crops in India.

Monsoon winds blow the strongest in southern Asia, but they also affect other parts of the world, including North America, West Africa, and northern Australia.

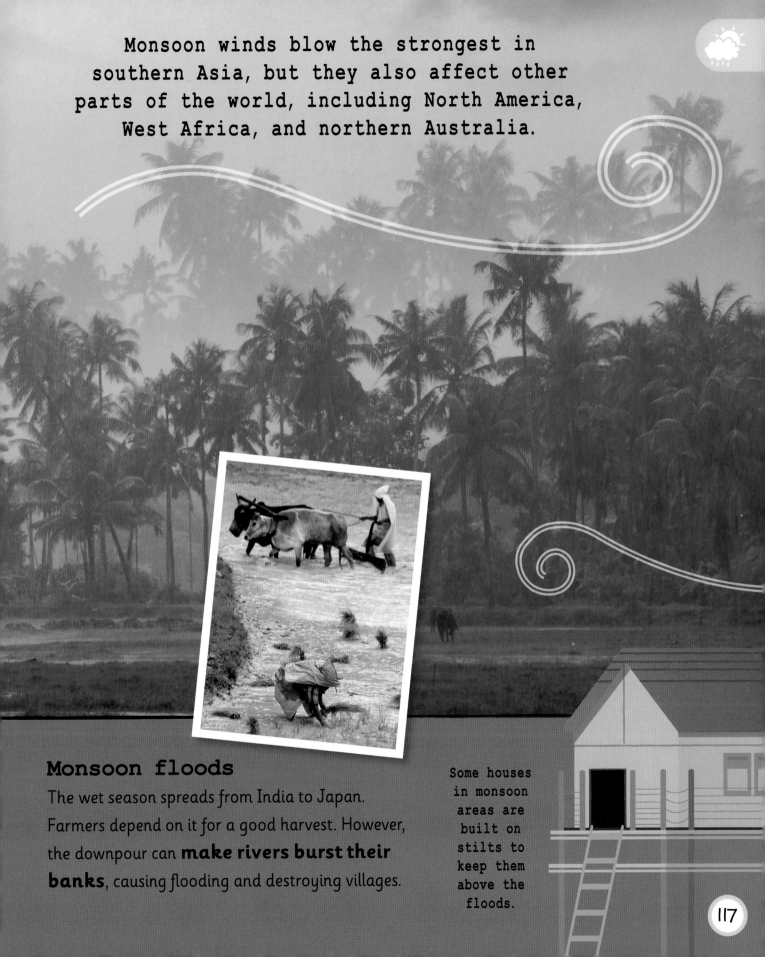

Monsoon floods

The wet season spreads from India to Japan. Farmers depend on it for a good harvest. However, the downpour can **make rivers burst their banks**, causing flooding and destroying villages.

Some houses in monsoon areas are built on stilts to keep them above the floods.

What is wind?

From gentle breezes to powerful gales, wind is **air moving** in different directions at different speeds. We feel the wind and we see things blowing in it.

Flowing air

When air flows over a warm area, it **heats up**. The **warm air then rises**, leaving space below for **cold air to flow in** and replace it. This flow of air is called **wind**.

Wind turbines

Wind power

People have used the power of the wind since ancient times. **Wind turbines** use the wind's energy to make **electricity**.

Wind god

In ancient Greek stories, the Anemoi were four wind gods: Boreas (north wind), Zephyros (west wind), Notos (south wind), and Euros (east wind).

Sandstorm, Arizona

Wind can blow large amounts of sand, and it can carry the sand over very long distances.

Wind and weather

Winds have an impact on the weather. They **carry cold air** into hot areas, changing the temperature. They can also **blow sand**, **dust**, or **snow**, covering the landscape in a new layer and sometimes causing damage.

Beaufort wind scale

The **strength** of the wind is measured by the Beaufort wind scale. This scale numbers each level of wind and describes what sort of **activity** each level causes.

0	Smoke rises straight up
1	Smoke drifts gently
2	Leaves rustle
3	Twigs move
4	Small branches move
5	Small trees sway
6	Umbrellas hard to use
7	Whole trees sway
8	Difficulty walking
9	Roofs damaged
10	Trees blown down
11	Houses damaged
12	Buildings destroyed

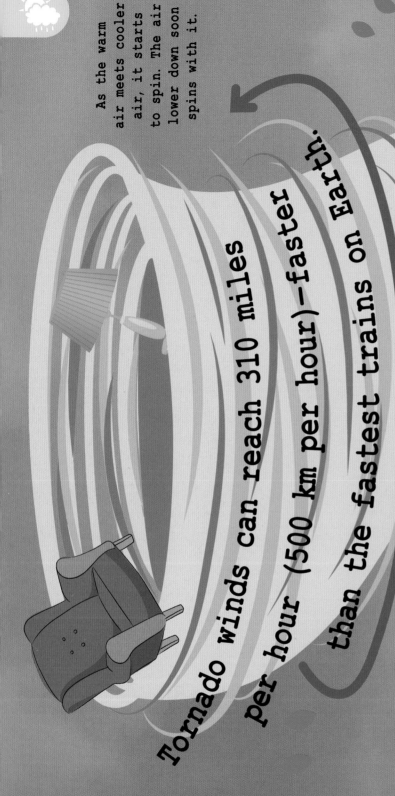

As the warm air meets cooler air, it starts to spin. The air lower down soon spins with it.

Warm, moist air rises up.

Tornado winds can reach 310 miles per hour (500 km per hour)—faster than the fastest trains on Earth.

Tornadoes

A tornado is a wind that spins at such a **ferocious speed** that everything in its path gets sucked up, flung around, or destroyed altogether. Tornadoes are the **fastest winds** in the world!

Whirling vortex

Tornadoes rage across the land. They develop when warm, moist air rises and spins, creating a **funnel-shaped cloud**. The funnel cloud grows bigger and reaches down to the ground, where the air rotates at **breakneck speed**.

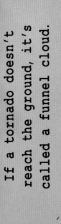

If a tornado doesn't reach the ground, it's called a funnel cloud.

Help! In a severe tornado, my feathers could be completely blown off! This has happened to chickens before.

Tornadoes are also called twisters.

Tornado damage

Tornadoes leave a **trail of destruction**. They can lift cars, people, and animals off the ground. Roofs fly off houses and power lines are blown down.

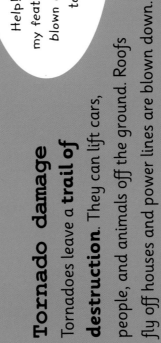

Tornadoes that happen at sea are called waterspouts. They drag sea water into spinning columns of spray, which suck up anything in their way.

Tornado Alley

The central states of the United States are known as Tornado Alley—they have around **1,000 tornadoes a year.** People stay safe in underground shelters or reinforced safe rooms until the tornado passes.

We'll stay safe until the tornado passes.

Underground shelter

SAFETY NOTE: Remember, NEVER go outside in tornado winds. Stay in a safe shelter.

Hurricanes

Hurricanes are given names like people. For example, Hurricane Katrina hit the southern United States in 2005.

Watch out! Dangerous hurricanes are **huge**, **spinning tropical storms**. They bring powerful winds and heavy rain.

Hurricanes can be wider than some countries!

Fast winds swirl and the hurricane spins.

Cold air flows in.

Strong winds blow up huge waves on the ocean's surface.

Growing a hurricane

Hurricanes start as thunderstorms over warm oceans. As warm air rises, cooler air flows in to replace it, making winds blow. Affected by Earth spinning on its axis, these winds begin to **swirl around** and a hurricane forms.

Eye of the storm

A hurricane's wild winds rage around a **safe**, **calm center**, called the eye of the storm.

The fastest winds and heaviest rains happen in the ring of cloud around the center of the hurricane.

Rain clouds are created.

Warm air rises up.

In some places HURRICANES are called TYPHOONS and in other parts of the world they are called CYCLONES. All three words mean the same thing.

5 Major destruction and flooding

4 Major damage and flooding

3 Some major damage

2 More severe damage

1 Some damage to buildings and trees

Saffir-Simpson scale

When a hurricane hits the coast, it devastates the land. The Saffir-Simpson scale gives hurricanes a number based on their wind speed and the level of damage they cause.

Wildfires

During long periods of hot weather with no rain, **uncontrollable wildfires** can break out and spread at high speed.

Rising temperatures

Temperatures are rising due to human activities, and this **climate change** means that wildfires are happening **more often**.

> In 2020, wildfires burned an area of land the size of ten million soccer fields.

Dry lands

Wildfires are common in Australia, South Africa, and the US. **Heatwaves** or **droughts** in forests and grasslands leave land so dry that the sun's heat, lightning, or a spark from human activities can start a fire.

It only takes one spark to start a wildfire. Winds spread them farther. Sometimes these fires only stop

Fighting fire

When fires break out, a **quick response** is essential to stop them from getting out of hand. **Aircraft** and **helicopters** drop water and chemicals to put out the fires, and thousands of **firefighters** work on the ground.

Wildlife

Some **animals die** in wildfires, but **many escape** by flying, running, or hiding. Those that leave must find new homes. Over time, the **trees** and **plants** in burned areas will **grow back**.

People try to save animals in danger from wildfires. Koalas have been rescued in Australia's bushland.

Mapping the weather

Weather maps give a **forecast** of the coming weather in different locations. This helps people to plan their activities and be prepared if weather warnings are looming!

Showing the weather

Weather maps show the weather in a local area or across a wider region, such as a whole country. You can view them on apps, on TV, or in newspapers, and find out what weather to expect.

Map symbols

Little pictures, including the **sun**, **clouds**, **snow**, or **rain clouds**, show the weather on a weather map.

Scientists who study weather are called meteorologists. Weather stations are places where experts monitor the weather.

Temperatures are shown as numbers in Fahrenheit (°F) or Celsius (°C).

85°F

Red lines and half-circles show areas of warm air. The half-circles point in the direction that the warm air is heading.

Blue lines and triangles show areas of cold air. The triangles point in the direction that the cold air is traveling.

Circular lines on weather maps are called isobars. They link areas with the same air pressure. The closer together the isobars are, the windier it will be.

The first weather forecast was published in an American newspaper in 1869.

Weather balloons are sent up into the sky with special instruments that gather information about the weather.

Science of weather

Meteorologists use **scientific instruments** to collect information about **temperature**, **air pressure**, and **wind speed**. This information is entered into computer systems that help scientists predict the weather.

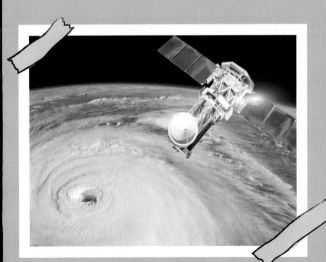

Satellites circling the Earth take photos that help meteorologists figure out what weather is coming.

Habitats

From dry deserts to waterlogged wetlands, the world has many habitats. A habitat is an environment **where an animal or plant naturally lives**. Each habitat provides shelter, space, food, and water. Wildlife adapts to survive in different habitats.

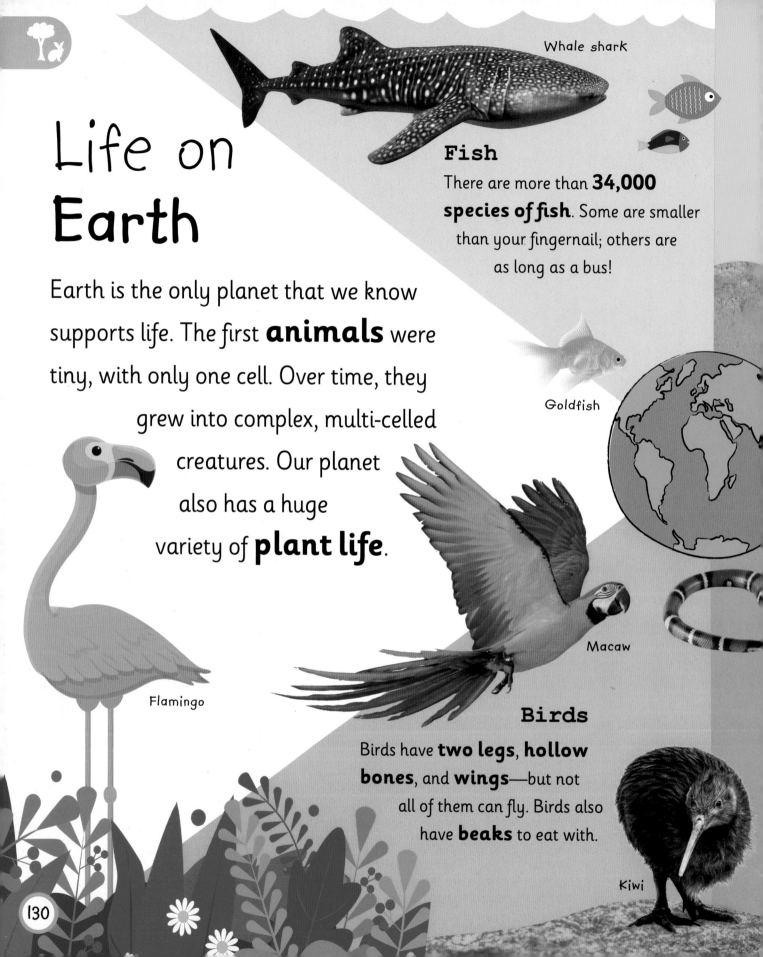

Life on Earth

Earth is the only planet that we know supports life. The first **animals** were tiny, with only one cell. Over time, they grew into complex, multi-celled creatures. Our planet also has a huge variety of **plant life**.

Whale shark

Fish
There are more than **34,000 species of fish**. Some are smaller than your fingernail; others are as long as a bus!

Goldfish

Flamingo

Macaw

Birds
Birds have **two legs, hollow bones**, and **wings**—but not all of them can fly. Birds also have **beaks** to eat with.

Kiwi

Amphibians

Amphibians are **cold-blooded** animals. Most amphibians spend part of their lives **in water** and part **on land**.

Frog

Salamander

Mammals

Mammals are **warm-blooded** animals that feed on their **mothers' milk** when they are young. There are more than **5,000 types of mammals**.

Monkey

Hamster and hamster pups

Plants

Animals, including humans, could not live without plants. Plants give off **oxygen**, and provide **food and homes** for animals. Humans also use plants for medicine and building materials.

Invertebrates

Animals **without a backbone** are called invertebrates. There are more than **one million invertebrate species** in the world. Most of these are insects.

Bees

Milk snake

Octopus

Reptiles

Reptiles are **scaly** animals that **lay eggs** to reproduce. They are **cold-blooded**, so they tend to live in warm areas.

Gecko

Climate

Weather is an event, like **rain** or **sunshine**, which happens over hours, days, or weeks. **Climate** is the **usual sort of weather** a place has over many years.

Types of climate

The sun's rays hit Earth at different angles in different places. This affects climate. Earth's main types of climate include: **tropical**, **subtropical**, **temperate**, and **polar**.

Tropical climates lie near the equator—an imaginary line around the middle of Earth. They experience hot temperatures and a lot of rain. They have no winter.

Subtropical climates are found north and south of the equator. They are often dry, with hot summers and mild winters.

Temperate climates have warm summers and cold winters. They also have four seasons: spring, summer, fall, and winter.

Polar climates are found at the top and bottom of the world. They are freezing cold all year round.

Earth's climate has always changed, but human activity is speeding up the changes and making them more extreme.

Climate change

Human activity is affecting our planet's climate. Burning fossil fuels, such as coal, releases **toxic gases** into the atmosphere. These gases **trap heat** on Earth, the same way a greenhouse traps heat, making the climate warmer. This is likely to lead to more extreme weather.

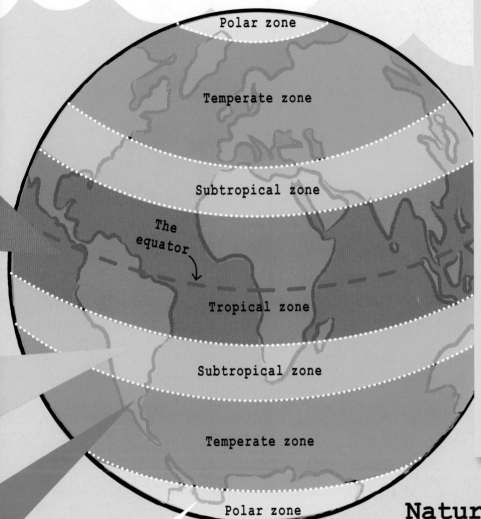

Polar zone

Temperate zone

Subtropical zone

The equator

Tropical zone

Subtropical zone

Temperate zone

Polar zone

Natural effects

As well as the sun, **oceans**, **mountains**, and **wind** are natural factors that impact climate. They affect how cold air and warm air move around our planet, and cause different places to experience different climates.

Near the ocean coast, it is cooler and wetter than areas farther away from the ocean.

Living together

An **ecosystem** is all the living things in a particular place and the way they affect each other and their surroundings. Each living thing plays a **role** in keeping the ecosystem **healthy**.

Food chain

A food chain shows how **energy** moves from one living thing to another in an ecosystem. The living things are either producers, consumers, or decomposers in the food chain.

The arrows show the direction of the flow of energy.

Grass grows using energy from the sun, and water and nutrients in the soil. It is a **producer**.

A **rabbit** eats the grass. It is a **primary consumer**.

A **fox** eats the rabbit. It is a **secondary consumer**.

Three roles

Producer, **consumer**, and **decomposer** are the three roles within an ecosystem.

1

Plants are producers. They make their own food using energy from the sun. Plants also need water, and they get nutrients from the soil.

2

Animals are consumers. They eat plants and other animals.

3

Bacteria and other tiny organisms are decomposers. They break down the waste from plants and animals.

Bacteria eats the bear's poop. It is a **decomposer**. Decomposers release nutrients into the soil, which help plants grow.

Nothing eats me, although they might eat my poop...

A **bear** eats the fox. It is a **tertiary consumer**. Tertiary consumers are at the top of food chains.

Deserts

There are **cold deserts** as well as **hot deserts**, but all deserts get **very little rain**. The **Sahara** is a hot desert in northern Africa. Here animals have adapted to survive the scorching temperatures.

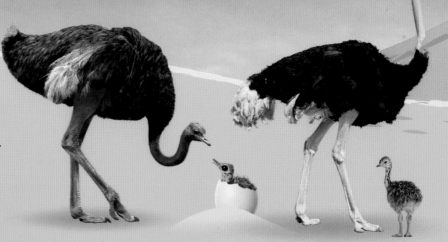

Ostrich

Ostriches cannot fly, but they can **run very fast**. Their eyes are protected from sandstorms by their thick eyelashes.

Wild desert gourd

Desert grass

Deathstalker scorpion

The deathstalker has enough **venom** to kill a small child. Its color keeps it **hidden** on the sand so it can hunt without being seen.

The Sahara has sand dunes, mountains, and rocky plains. It is baking hot here in the daytime, but at night, it can be freezing.

Arabian camel

The Arabian camel can travel miles in the desert **without water**. It stores **fat** in its one hump. The fat keeps it going when food is scarce.

Arabian camels are also known as dromedaries.

Sand viper

These snakes **bury themselves** in the sand. This protects them from the sun and lets them surprise their prey.

Desert plants

Desert plants must be able to **live without much water**, sometimes for months or years at a time.

Palm tree

Dung beetle

This beetle **eats poop**! It uses its good sense of smell to find dung in the desert. Some dung beetles roll the poop into balls. They can roll the balls to their nests.

Grasslands

Grasslands are **vast**, **open areas** covered with **wild grasses**. They can also be called savannas, prairies, steppes, pampas, and velds.

The Serengeti is home to many grazing plant eaters like us.

The Serengeti
The **Serengeti**, in east-central Africa, is one of the world's largest savannas. It is home to many animals, including giraffes, zebras, and lions.

Zebra
The zebra's **striped, black-and-white coat** makes it hard for predators to pick out one zebra from a group.

Lion
Lions are **fierce predators** in the Serengeti, **hunting prey** such as zebras and wildebeest. Male and female lions hunt, but females do most of the hunting for their family group.

Every year, more than 1.5 million wildebeest travel across the Serengeti. They walk huge distances in search of new grazing areas and water. Other animals, such as zebras, join them.

Grassland plants

As well as different **grasses** and **wildflowers**, **scattered trees** and **shrubs** grow in grasslands.

Elephant

Elephants feed on the grasses and tree leaves in the Serengeti. These gentle giants are the **largest animals** on land.

Acacia tree

Black rhinoceros

The Serengeti's black rhinoceros has **two horns**. It uses them to battle rival rhinos, fight off enemies such as lions, and to dig up roots to eat.

Wetlands

Wetlands are areas of **very wet land**. They include marshes, mangroves, swamps, and bogs. The **Everglades** is a wetland in southern Florida. It's a swampy, very slow-moving river.

Mangrove trees

Mosquito

These **blood-sucking bugs** thrive in the Everglades. They can spread a dangerous disease called malaria.

Wetland plants

Wetland plants are able to grow **in wet soil** or **in water**. They include mangrove trees, orchids, grasses, and shrubs.

Grasses

Ghost orchid

The Everglades is a great place for frogs and toads. The southern chorus frog mostly comes out at night, but can be seen in the daytime. It makes a noisy, chirping call.

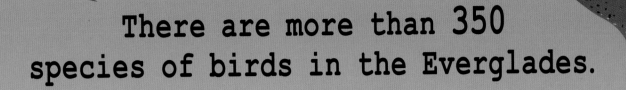

There are more than 350 species of birds in the Everglades.

Our pink coloring comes from the algae and shrimp we eat.

American flamingo

This pink bird has **long legs** for wading in the Everglades water, and **webbed feet** for swimming. It finds food in the water, such as algae and shrimp, and feeds by filtering the water through its beak.

Watch out for alligators like me! Around 200,000 alligators live in the Everglades!

Alligator

These large reptiles have **long tails** and **powerful jaws**. They hide in shallow water, waiting to catch fish, birds, and other animals. **Snap!**

Florida box turtle

This turtle **does not like to swim**. Instead, it lives by the Everglades water under bushes. It eats insects, leaves, and fruit.

Deciduous woodlands

These forests are green in spring and summer, and yellow, red, orange, and brown in fall when deciduous trees start to **lose their leaves**. In winter, the tree branches are bare. **Białowieża** (say: bee-ah-wo-vee-edge-ah) is an ancient deciduous forest in Poland.

Dormouse

The dormouse is found in deciduous woodlands. It's a **good climber** and is active at night, looking for food. During winter, it **hibernates** (goes into a deep sleep).

Grass snake

Feeding on woodland frogs and toads, grass snakes often **live close to water**.

As well as deciduous trees such as beech and oak, plants here include lichens, mosses, and fungi, such as mushrooms.

My beak makes a loud knock-knock-knock sound as I peck the tree.

White-backed woodpecker

Woodpeckers drill their **strong beaks** into the woodland tree trunks to find food such as insects, and to make nests.

European bison

Long ago, bison were widespread in Europe. Białowieża is one place in Europe where bison still roam freely today. Bison **live in herds**. They eat grasses, shoots, and leaves.

Eurasian lynx

The Eurasian lynx **hunts at night**. It sneaks up on its woodland prey, then jumps on it.

I'm getting out of here!

Rainforests

Rainforests are **hot**, **wet places** that are home to around half of Earth's plant and animal species. The **Amazon rainforest** in South America is buzzing with life.

Macaw

Brazil nut tree

Passion flower

Rainforest plants

The Amazon is home to a **huge variety of plants**, including Brazil nut trees, passion flowers, strangler figs, and rubber trees.

Strangler fig

Rubber tree

Jaguar

The jaguar prowls through the rainforest. It **hunts at night** and can crush the skulls of large mammals in its powerful jaws.

The equator

Rainforests are found around the equator. They stay warm and wet all year.

Harpy eagle

This powerful bird **hunts high up** in the rainforest, in the **tops of the trees**. It snatches monkeys and sloths with its fearsome talons (claws).

Howler monkey

This rainforest monkey is the **loudest creature** on land. It also has an **amazing nose**—it can smell food from a long way away.

Blue morpho butterfly

Three-toed sloth

This sloth's life revolves around **eating leaves** and **sleeping**. It lives mostly in the rainforest trees, coming down to the ground to poop.

Green anaconda

Leafcutter ant

These ants **bite off leaf pieces** from rainforest plants and carry them to their colony for food. They can carry more than fifty times their own body weight.

Tarantula

Golden dart frog

Evergreen forests

Evergreen forests stay **green all year round** because evergreen trees do not lose their leaves in winter. Canada's **Alberta Mountain** forests are home to many evergreen trees and large mammals.

Plants

Pine, **spruce**, and **cedar trees** grow here. Other plant life includes **orchids**, **ferns**, and **lichens**.

Moose

Moose live in the Alberta Mountain forests. Their **long legs** help them to walk in water and snow. Males have **large antlers**, which they use to fight off rival moose in the mating season.

Bald eagle

This eagle **looks for prey** as it flies through the trees. It hunts other birds, small mammals, and fish. It also steals food from other eagles.

Evergreen forests can be found in coastal areas that have mild winters, and in inland areas with dry climates, such as the Alberta Mountains.

American pygmy shrew

This **tiny forest mammal** is around the length of your thumb (including its tail!). It only lives for around thirteen months.

Gray wolf

Wolves thrive in the evergreen forests, living in **packs** with up to thirty members. They **howl** to bring the pack together.

Grizzly bear

These bears dig their **homes (called dens)** in the ground of the Alberta Mountain forests. They **hibernate** (go into a deep sleep) during winter, for up to seven months.

147

Tundra

In tundra areas, it **rarely rains** and the ground is **frozen** for most of the year. In the **Siberian tundra** in northern Asia, plants and animals have to be tough to survive.

Arctic ground squirrel

This squirrel digs a **shallow shelter** in thawed tundra ground. It **hibernates** here, sleeping away the freezing winter.

Plants here are short in height. This helps them avoid bitter tundra winds.

← Flowers

← Grasses

Tundra plants

Tundra means "**treeless**"—very few trees grow in this habitat. There are other plants though, including flowers, grasses, lichens, and small shrubs.

Lichen

The tundra has two seasons: a long winter of around ten months and a short summer.

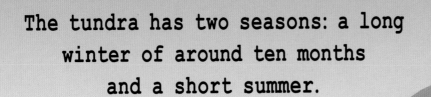

Reindeer

Reindeer have **large hooves** that help them to walk on tundra snow and paddle through rivers and lakes.

Siberian crane

This crane **wades** in **shallow water** in the tundra and dips its whole head under the water's surface to feed.

Brown lemming

This **small rodent** does not hibernate like other tundra mammals. In the winter months, it's **busy digging** for mosses and roots to eat.

Mountain living

Mountains are **harsh environments**. Animals and plants in the **Himalayas**, in central Asia, cope with strong winds and freezing temperatures.

Yak
Yaks have **thick, shaggy coats** to keep them warm.

Himalayan marmot
Cute but **tasty**, marmots are a key meal for many mountain predators, including wolves and brown bears.

Moss

Lichen

Snow leopard
This **endangered leopard** can jump up to six times its body length. It has **thick fur**, which helps it stay warm in the cold mountains.

Trees grow lower down in the mountains, but high up where it's colder only mosses, lichens, and grasses grow.

Lammergeier
This mountain bird is a **scavenger**—it eats the meat of animals that are already dead.

Siberian ibex
These wild goats are **great mountain climbers**. They can even climb steep crags.

Pine trees

Pika
These **little mountain mammals** are related to hares and rabbits.

I eat grasses, thistles, and lichens.

Freezing poles

The world has two polar regions. They are **icy**, **remote places**, where seawater freezes, and very few plants can grow. **Antarctica** is the polar region at the bottom of our planet. It's a frozen continent.

Antarctic blue whale

The **largest creature on Earth**, the Antarctic blue whale weighs the same as thirty-three elephants and is longer than two buses.

I eat loads and loads of tiny krill.

Antarctic krill

Krill are **small shellfish** that live in **large swarms** in the ocean around Antarctica. They are eaten by bigger creatures, such as whales.

A swarm of krill

The ice that covers most of the continent of Antarctica is extremely thick.

The Adelie penguin is found throughout Antarctica. Like all penguins, it lives in groups called colonies.

Arctic

Antarctica

The Arctic is the polar region at the top of the world. It contains a frozen sea and parts of several countries.

Antarctica is the polar region at the bottom of the world. It's a continent and almost completely covered in ice.

Egg

Emperor penguin

The male emperor penguin stays on the Antarctic ice for two months, **keeping his partner's egg warm** and **safe**. He doesn't eat anything during this time!

I can dive down and down—really deep in the water.

Antarctica is the coldest of the two polar regions.

Crabeater seal

Despite their name, these Antarctic seals **don't eat crabs**. Instead, they dive into the freezing water to feed on krill.

Leopard seal

This fierce Antarctic predator has **sharp teeth** and **powerful jaws**. It hides near penguin colonies and grabs its victims as they enter the water.

Ocean temperatures

Earth's oceans aren't all the same temperature. In the **polar regions**, the water is **freezing**. Near the **equator**, it is fairly **warm**. These different temperatures suit different plants and animals.

Warm water

Lionfish
The lionfish **prefers warm waters** around coral reefs. However, it **can live in colder waters**, too.

Green sea turtle
Like all turtles, these large sea turtles are cold-blooded. They **live in tropical waters**, where they can stay warm.

Orca
This whale has layers of fat that keep it warm **in cold water**. It can also keep cool **in warm water** by letting heat escape from its skin.

Warm water plants

Seagrass   Rockweed

Group of orcas

Warm waters near the equator

Freezing waters in polar regions

We orcas are happy in water of any temperature, warm or cold.

Cold water plants

Sargassum is a seaweed that floats in large mats in an area called the Sargasso Sea.

Kelp is a large, brown seaweed.

Cold water

Greenland shark

Walrus

A thick layer of fat, called **blubber**, helps walruses stay warm **in freezing Arctic waters**.

Greenland shark

This shark lives **deep below freezing sea ice**. To stay warm, it can make its blood temperature warmer than the water it is swimming in.

Polar bear

This **Arctic bear** swims from one place to another **in icy waters**. It has a layer of fat, a warm fur coat, and rough paws to grip slippery ice.

Coral reefs

Coral reefs are **huge**, **colorful habitats** found in **warm seas**. They support a great variety of life. Australia's **Great Barrier Reef** is the largest reef system in the world.

Coral polyps

Coral polyps

Coral reefs are made up of millions of **tiny, cup-like creatures** called polyps.

The outer layer of the reef is alive. The inner layers are made of dead coral skeletons.

I'm the daddy and I'm guarding my babies!

Clownfish

These **striped fish** live in coral reefs. After the female clownfish lays her eggs, the male clownfish **guards them** until they hatch.

Clownfish eggs

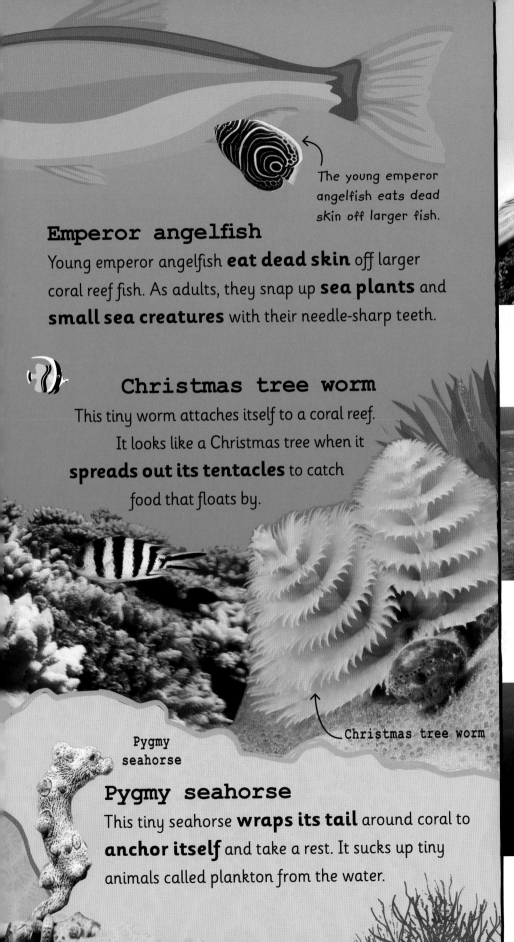

The young emperor angelfish eats dead skin off larger fish.

Emperor angelfish

Young emperor angelfish **eat dead skin** off larger coral reef fish. As adults, they snap up **sea plants** and **small sea creatures** with their needle-sharp teeth.

Christmas tree worm

This tiny worm attaches itself to a coral reef. It looks like a Christmas tree when it **spreads out its tentacles** to catch food that floats by.

Christmas tree worm

Pygmy seahorse

Pygmy seahorse

This tiny seahorse **wraps its tail** around coral to **anchor itself** and take a rest. It sucks up tiny animals called plankton from the water.

Coral reefs

There are **several types** of coral reefs.

Fringing reefs are near coastlines.

Barrier reefs are separated from land by an area of water.

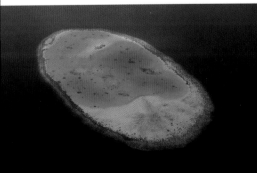

Atolls are rings of reef in the open ocean.

157

Ocean layers

The ocean is divided into **five layers** called **zones**.

All sorts of **amazing creatures** live in each zone.

As you travel deeper in the ocean, light fades, temperatures drop, and the weight of water above increases.

We green sea turtles dive down to eat plants that live in the sunlit zone. We swim up to the water's surface to breathe.

Seaweed

Seaweed **needs light** from the sun to grow. It can only survive in the shallow **sunlit zone**.

Most sea creatures live in the sunlit zone.

Giant hatchetfish

This fish has **huge eyes** that point upward, helping it spot prey in the dim light of the **twilight zone**.

No plants grow in the bottom four zones.

Sunlit zone

Twilight zone

Anglerfish

This fish hunts in the pitch-black **midnight zone**. It has a **long strand growing from its head**, with a **glowing bulb** at the end to attract the sea creatures it eats.

Gulper eel

This eel's **mouth** can grow into a **large, floppy bag**. This helps it gulp up tiny fish from the cold, black waters of the **abyssal zone**.

Snailfish

These fish can live in the **hadal zone**, which contains the deepest waters on Earth. Snailfish have a **soft skeleton** to survive the **intense pressure** at these depths.

In the hadal zone, the deepest spot on Earth is in the Mariana Trench in the Pacific Ocean. It's called the Challenger Deep.

Midnight zone   Abyssal zone   Hadal zone   159

Deep-sea smokers

Deep-sea smokers are **openings** in the seafloor. They spew out **superhot water** containing **minerals** that support living things. The minerals solidify, creating towering structures.

Ear-like fin

Dumbo octopus

Dumbo octopus

Some species of dumbo octopus live around deep-sea smokers. They **feed on the creatures there**, such as **clams** and **crabs**.

Deep down in the ocean, deep-sea smokers support an amazing web of life.

Microbes

Microbes (**tiny living things**) on the seafloor **eat the minerals** from deep-sea smokers. Creatures such as shrimp, mussels, and clams then eat the microbes.

Microbes

Life on Earth probably began in places like these around 4.3 billion years ago.

Deep-sea smokers can be as tall as buildings.

Shrimp

Giant clams

Giant worm

White shrimp

Small shrimp **feed on the microbes** around deep-sea smokers. These shrimp are often blind.

Giant clams

Giant clams survive by **sucking in the mineral-rich water** from deep-sea smokers.

I'm a hungry giant clam. More minerals for me, please! Slurp!

Giant worms

Giant worms live around the bases of deep-sea smokers. They are as **long** and **thick as a human arm**.

City life

Cities are a **human habitat**, where a lot of people live close together. But humans are not the only animals that call cities home.

Seagull

Fig tree

City plants

Trees and plants vary from one city to the next. The trees, shrubs, and flowers in parks and gardens provide **great habitats for animals.**

Squirrels

Grasshopper

Rats

Black and brown rats live in **sewers**, around **trash bins**, and **under homes**. They have long tails, muscular bodies, and sharp teeth that grow constantly.

Grass

Cockroach

Brown rats

Pigeons

These birds live in nearly every city in the world. They build their **nests** in **house gutters**, **chimneys**, and **wall ledges**. Pigeons eat a variety of foods, including seeds, berries, and food waste.

Oak tree

Bat

Pigeons

Humans

Humans are **intelligent**, **social animals** that like to live together in **groups**. Humans also live with other animals, such as dogs and cats.

Human

Cat

Butterflies

Dog

Red foxes

Red foxes run wild in European cities and are considered pests. They hunt through **human garbage**, looking for food, and often build their **homes (called dens) under garden sheds**.

Red fox

Human planet

Over thousands of years, humans have been changing the world. We have learned to build shelters, grow food, keep animals as farm animals, and make the things we need. This has made us the **dominant species on Earth**. Today, our planet is one large human habitat.

1 Hunters and gatherers

The first humans used **stone tools**. They lived in groups and **moved around** to **hunt animals** and **gather plants** to eat.

2 First farmers

Around 12,000 years ago, humans began to live in **set places**. They learned how to **grow food** and **raise animals**. These humans were the first farmers.

People of Earth

Modern humans have been around for **hundreds of thousands of years**. During this time, our numbers have grown from a handful of people to a population of nearly **eight billion**.

3 Early cities

Over time, groups of farms grew into **villages**. Some villages then grew into **cities**. The buildings were made of mud, brick, and stone.

Remains of an early settlement in Turkey

4 Empires

Around 4,300 years ago, leaders started to rule over **vast lands**, called empires. Leaders of empires used **armies** to **keep their power over people**.

The Temple of Philae in Egypt was built during the time of the ancient Egyptian civilization.

The spinning room in a rope-making factory, around 1885, Shadwell, UK

5 Industry begins

Around 200 years ago, the **Industrial Revolution** started. **Machines** were invented that could make **a lot of products** more quickly than ever before.

We've come a long way since stone tools!

6 The world today

Today, there are nearly **200 countries** in the world. **Technology** allows us to send messages and images across our planet instantly, and even fly to other worlds in outer space.

Earth's resources

The Earth has many natural resources that humans use. These include **air**, **water**, **plants**, **minerals**, and **fossil fuels**.

Sunlight

Renewable resources

Many of the natural resources humans use are renewable. This means they **cannot be used up**. Renewable resources include **water**, **air**, and **sunlight**.

Water

Air

Living things
Plants and **animals reproduce** to keep their species alive. This makes them a **renewable resource**.

New wheat will grow from the wheat seeds.

Non-renewable resources
Non-renewable resources form over millions of years. They include **fossil fuels**, **minerals**, and **stone**. They **can run out** because humans are using them up faster than they form.

Potassium

Terbium and dysprosium are rare Earth elements that are

Fossil fuels

Fossil fuels, such as **coal**, **oil**, and **gas**, are **non-renewable**. Humans burn fossil fuels for cooking and heating, to create electricity, and to power vehicles. However, burning them is causing **climate change**.

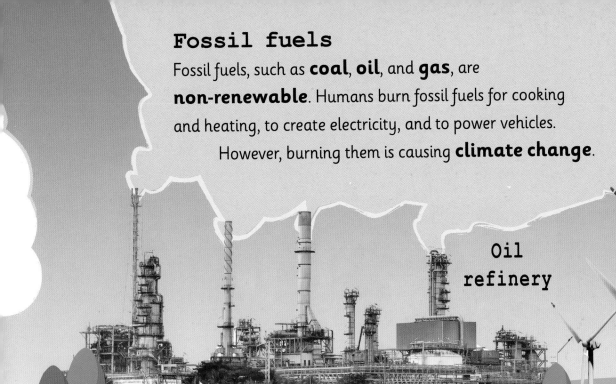

Oil refinery

Clean resources

To help slow down climate change, we can use **clean renewable energy** instead of fossil fuels. For instance, we can use **solar panels** to capture the sun's energy or **wind turbines** that use the wind to make power.

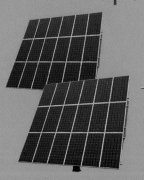

Solar panels

Wind turbines

Non-renewable resources often form under the ground.

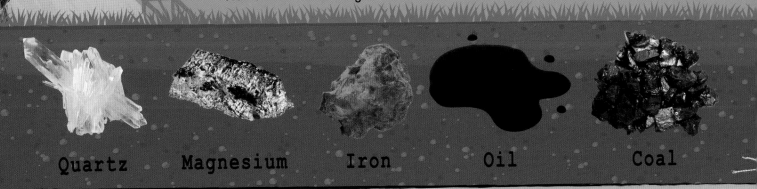

Quartz   Magnesium   Iron   Oil   Coal

used in cell phone screens. They are non-renewable.

Farming

Farms are where people **grow crops** and **raise animals**. They provide the food that people eat. There are many different types of farms.

Farm products range from meat to coffee beans, and include non-food crops such as flowers or cotton.

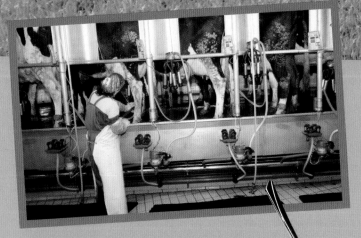

Dairy farms

Dairy farmers raise **cows**. They sell **cow's milk** and **meat**. The milk is also used to make products, such as butter, cheese, and yogurt.

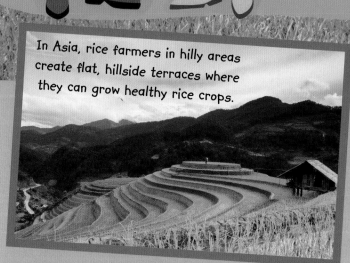

In Asia, rice farmers in hilly areas create flat, hillside terraces where they can grow healthy rice crops.

Arable farms

On arable farms, farmers **grow crops** such as **grains** and **legumes**. Grain crops such as corn, wheat, and rice are grown in huge quantities around the world.

Fruit orchards

Orchards are places where **fruit trees** are grown, such as orange, apple, and cherry trees. The **fruit** is picked and then packed and sent to stores.

Farming and climate change

We need farms for food, but farming has an **impact on our planet**. For example, farm animals such as cows release methane, which is one of the gases that causes **climate change**.

Excuse me!

Poultry farms

Poultry farmers raise birds, including chickens and ducks. They sell the **birds' eggs** and **meat**. On free-range poultry farms, birds can roam outside.

Greenhouse growing

Greenhouses stay warm, and allow **fruit** and **vegetables** to be grown **all year round**.

Fishing

People have been fishing for tens of thousands of years. Today, vast numbers of fish and other sea creatures are **caught as food**. Some people also fish for fun.

Spear

First fishing
The first people to fish used **spears**, **nets**, and **lines**. Today, people still use these methods to **catch fish for their families**.

Fishing rods

Small fishing boat

Outboard motor

Fishing net

Small fishing boats
People use small fishing boats to **catch seafood for their village** or to **sell at markets**. These boats are equipped with oars, sails, or outboard motors, and fishing nets.

More than 9.1 million tons of fish a year are

Trawlers

Trawlers are **large fishing ships** that **catch seafood** by **dragging huge nets** through the water. The nets can damage seabed habitats, and animals such as dolphins, seals, and turtles get caught in them and drown.

Trawler

Huge fishing net

Fish farms

Some fish, such as **salmon**, **cod**, and **tuna**, can be raised on fish farms. The fish are kept in **cages** in shallow coastal waters. They have to be fed, just like farm animals on land.

Cage for fish farming

Protecting fish

Overfishing has caused some species of fish to become **extinct**. **Sustainable fishing** can help stop this by leaving enough fish in the sea to keep fish populations at a healthy level, and by taking care of fish and their habitats.

I'm an orange roughy and there's not many of my species left because we have been overfished.

caught by accident and thrown back into the water dead.

Mining and drilling

Mining is an industry in which **valuable rocks** and **minerals** are **dug up** from underground or from Earth's surface. **Drilling** is used to reach **liquid oil**.

Opencast mining

In opencast mines, **coal** or **minerals such as iron ore** are dug up from the **surface** of the ground. A machine called an **excavator** does the digging.

Coal mine

Shaft mining

In shaft mines, **vertical** or **near-vertical tunnels** go deep down underground. Miners use **elevators** to reach the tunnels.

Drilling for oil

To reach oil under the ground or below the seabed, a drill **cuts through rock** to create a **well**. Oil then flows out of the well.

The Bagger 288 is a ginormous excavator that digs out coal in an opencast mine.

Opencast mines are also called quarries.

RHEINBRAUN 288

KRUPP SIEMENS

An ordinary digger looks tiny next to the Bagger 288.

Drift mining

In drift mines, **horizontal tunnels** are dug into the side of a mountain or hill. Miners dig in the tunnels for coal or minerals such as quartz.

Panning for gold

Panning is a simple mining method. It has often been used for mining gold. A **shallow pan** is used to scoop **deposits** from a **riverbed**. The pan's contents are then **swirled**, so that heavier deposits, such as gold, sink to the bottom of the pan and can be picked out.

Industries

In industries, people **collect raw materials** such as coal, **make products** to sell, or **sell services** to other people. For example, products are made in factories and then sold, and people in restaurants and banks provide services.

This picture shows a Victorian flax mill that made yarn from the flax plant.

First factories

The first factories were built more than 200 years ago during the **Industrial Revolution**. Before there were factories, everything was made by hand.

Making products

Everything we buy has been **prepared** or **made by people**, or **people** and **machines**. For instance, bread is made in a bakery, and toys are made in factories.

Robotic arms can make cars all day and night without a break!

Robotic machines

In many modern factories, **robots operate machines** instead of humans.

Robotic arm

As well as filling the air with harmful smoke, this factory produces toxic waste, which pollutes my water.

Pollution

The first factories were powered by coal, and today many factories still use **fossil fuels**. These fuels **harm the environment**. Some industries are trying to use less harmful energy, such as wind or water power.

Service sector

Today, many people work in service jobs. They **provide a service**. For example, a car mechanic provides a service by fixing cars, and a teacher provides a service by teaching children.

$2 \times 12 = ?$

Transportation

Humans use transportation to **move themselves** and **their things** from one place to another. The first forms of transportation were boats, horses, and carts. We now have many types of transportation.

VSS Unity
(a spaceplane)

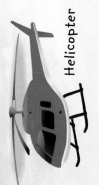

Helicopter

Planes and helicopters

Planes are used for traveling **long distances quickly.** Helicopters are used for **shorter trips.** In 2021, a **spaceplane** took its first passengers to the **edge of space.**

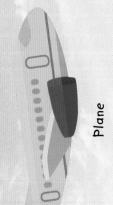

Plane

Ships

The **first boats** were **single-person canoes.** Today, we have a **huge range** of boats and ships. Enormous cruise ships take people on vacations.

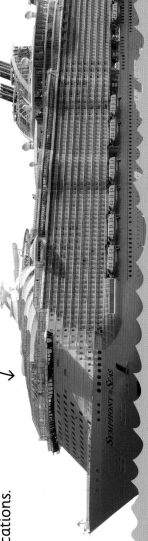

The cruise ship *Symphony of the Seas* can carry 6,680 passengers and has a park, 22 restaurants, and an ice-skating rink.

Electric car at a charging point

Steam train

The first trains were steam powered.

Steam engines burn fuel such as coal to heat water and make steam.

I'm riding a penny-farthing bicycle. It was invented around 150 years ago.

Trains

Trains run on **tracks**. They use **diesel** or **electricity** for fuel. Superfast maglev trains use magnetic forces to remove friction between the train and the track.

Bikes, cars, trucks, and trams travel on the roads.

Maglev passenger train

Road vehicles

Most cars and other road vehicles are powered by burning **fossil fuels** such as **diesel** or **petroleum**, which give off harmful gases. However, many road vehicles are now built with **electric engines**, which cause much less pollution.

Bicycles

Bicycles are **two-wheeled machines**. A rider pushes the pedals to make the wheels turn around.

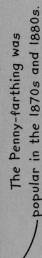

The Penny-farthing was popular in the 1870s and 1880s.

Towns and villages

People like to live in **groups**. Early humans lived together in caves and huts. These settlements grew into **villages**. Over time, villages became **towns** and **cities**. Do you live in a village, a town, or a city?

Village in Liping County, China

A **village** is made up of a **small group of houses** and other **buildings**, such as a school.

Around the world, village homes can be built from different materials.

A **town** is **bigger than a village**, with more people, houses, and streets. Towns also have businesses, such as banks, cafés, and supermarkets, and places of entertainment, such as movie theaters.

Winthrop, Washington

CASCADES OUTDOOR STORE

Village

Town

Polluting cities

Cities are some of the most polluting places on Earth. **Harmful gases** from vehicles, factories, and household heating can hang over cities as **smog**, which is bad for us to breathe in.

Smog is smoky fog.

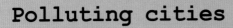

Ghaziabad, India

In the 1950s, New York City became the first megacity.

Berlin, Germany

Cities are **large towns**. They contain houses, stores, restaurants, schools, offices, high-rise buildings, factories, museums, theaters, parks, universities, and more.

A **megacity** is a **massive city** with a population of more than **ten million people**. The largest megacity is Tokyo, in Japan, which is home to more than thirty-seven million people.

Tokyo, Japan

City

Megacity

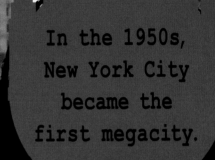

Language

People use language to **communicate**. They talk, write, or make gestures. There are more than **7,000 different languages** in the world.

Spoken languages

Different languages are spoken in different parts of the world. The **most widely spoken** languages are **Mandarin Chinese**, **English**, and **Spanish**.

Our ancestors developed language millions of years ago. Early languages may have been songlike, mostly gestures, or simple words.

Hola!
Spanish

Hello!
English

Nǐ hǎo!
Mandarin Chinese

Cuneiform was written on clay tablets.

Written language

The first written language was invented in **ancient Sumer** (modern day Iraq) around **5,000 years ago**. Made up of symbols and pictures, this language was called **cuneiform**.

Cuneiform tablet

Veni, vidi, vici.
(Latin for "I came, I saw, I conquered.")

The Roman general Julius Caesar made the above Latin phrase famous.

Sign languages

Hand signs, **facial expressions**, and **finger spelling** are used in sign languages to communicate. Many people who are deaf use sign languages.

Dead languages

Languages that are **no longer commonly used** are known as dead languages. **Latin** is considered to be a dead language. It was used by the **ancient Romans**.

Languages such as Italian, French, and Spanish have their roots in Latin.

more than one language.

Mapping our world

Maps are **drawings of our planet** that show areas as they would appear if we **looked down** on them **from above**. Maps teach us about our world.

Maps and globes

Making a flat map of the round Earth is like trying to **flatten out** the skin of an orange—you can't do it perfectly! To make flat maps, mapmakers have to **distort** things a little bit.

A ball-shaped object showing a map of the world is called a globe.

Some maps show invisible features, such as country borders.

Some maps show physical features, such as mountains or rivers.

Using a map

Maps show the distance between locations. They help us figure out **how to get to places**.

Today, we can look at maps on our cell phones.

Maps have a key that explains what the map's symbols mean.

A map's compass shows you which way is north, east, south, or west.

Key

Mountains

Forest

Path

Treasure

Scale

10 mi   20 mi   30 mi

1 in   2 in   3 in

Starting here, what physical features would you pass on your way to the treasure?

A map is always smaller than the place it is showing.
It shows how much smaller by displaying a scale line.
This shows what the smaller map measurements represent.

Save our planet!

Today, Earth is being polluted, its resources are running low, its forests are being destroyed, and its oceans are being contaminated. **Climate change** threatens our world. But by making changes, we can create a happy, healthy planet for future generations to enjoy.

People pressure

The world is experiencing a population explosion. With more people needing food, water, and shelter, there is more pressure on our planet's **limited resources**.

Population growth

The global population has rocketed from **one billion in 1800** to **almost eight billion in 2020**. This increases the demand for daily essentials, such as food, clothing, housing, and energy.

Population: nearly 8 billion

Population: 1 billion

1800

2020

Every hour the world's population grows by more than 8,000 people.

Pollution problems

With more people in the world, pollution levels are rising. **Factories** and **vehicles** are two causes of pollution. They can fill the air with toxic substances.

Habitat loss

Every year we lose forests, grasslands, and wetlands because they are **cleared** to make space for **farmland** or **buildings**. This destroys plant and animal habitats, and adds to climate change because trees absorb harmful carbon dioxide.

Protect the planet!

It is up to us to **take responsibility** for our actions on Earth and protect our planet for the people of the future.

Living longer

As well as growing, the population is **aging**. People are living longer than ever before because they have better lifestyles and medical treatment.

Climate **change**

Our planet is **heating up** at a faster rate than ever before and it is likely to experience **more extreme weather**. This climate change is mostly caused by human activities.

Greenhouse effect

Activities such as burning fossil fuels, farming animals, and cutting down trees increase the amount of **harmful gases** in Earth's atmosphere. These gases trap heat, **warming the Earth like a greenhouse**.

Less heat can escape into outer space. The trapped heat makes our planet warmer, and this is expected to lead to more extreme weather.

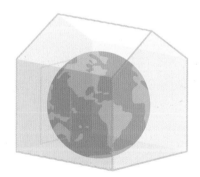

A greenhouse traps the sun's heat to keep plants warm. Gases such as carbon dioxide trap heat on Earth.

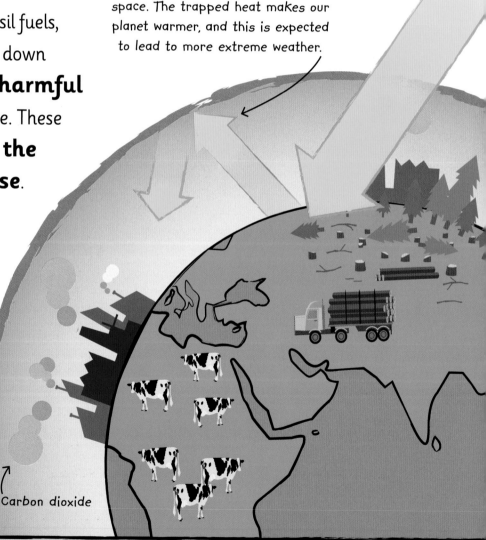

Carbon dioxide

Earth is expected to become around

Melting ice

At the North and South poles, higher temperatures are melting **glaciers** (slowly moving ice masses on land) and **sea ice** (frozen sea water). Many animals need these ice habitats to survive. For instance, polar bears hunt seals on sea ice.

Without Arctic sea ice, it's hard for polar bears to hunt.

Dry places are likely to get drier and wet places are likely to get wetter.

If sea levels rise, the land can flood.

Rising sea levels

As the huge glaciers on Earth's land melt, **sea levels rise**. This means millions of people who live along coastlines are at **risk of flooding**.

Loss of islands

As sea levels rise, low-lying islands may **disappear underwater**. The Maldives in the Indian Ocean could vanish within the next one hundred years.

The Maldives

4.5°F (2.5°C) hotter during the next one hundred years.

Fossil fuels

The most common fossil fuels are **coal**, **oil**, and **natural gas**. Most of the world's **energy** comes from burning these fuels, but burning them harms our planet.

CO_2
CO_2
CO_2
CO_2

Unless we use alternative energies, every time we turn on a light, watch TV, or ride in a car, we're using fossil fuels.

Fuel formation

Fossil fuels are formed from the **remains of ancient plants** and **animals**. They are found inside Earth's crust.

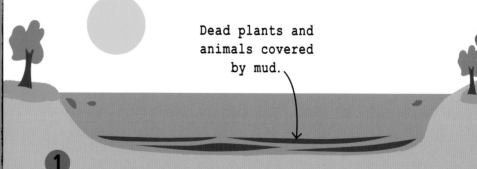

Dead plants and animals covered by mud.

1

Millions of years ago, the animals and plants that died in oceans and other water habitats were covered by mud.

Burning fossil fuels

Power stations burn coal, oil, or gas to make **electricity**, which we use for lighting, heating, and appliances. Gas is also burned for **heating** and **cooking**. Many **vehicles** burn fuel in their **engines**.

CO_2
CO_2
CO_2

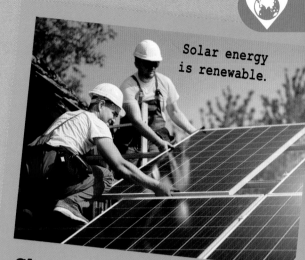

Solar energy is renewable.

Pollution problems

Burning fossil fuels releases the gas **carbon dioxide (CO_2)** into Earth's atmosphere, which adds to the greenhouse effect, leading to climate change.

Short supply

Earth has a limited supply of fossil fuels. Alternative sources of energy that are **clean** and **renewable** are essential to keep the world running, while also protecting the environment.

Power station

3 Over millions of years, heat and pressure changed the dead matter into natural gas, oil, and coal.

4 Today, we mine or drill for fossil fuels and use their energy.

2 The dead animals and plants were buried under more layers of mud and sand.

Natural gas

Oil

Coal

Renewable energy

Where can we find sources of energy that **won't run out** or harm the environment? The answer is just about **everywhere in nature!**

Energy forever

Fossil fuels are running out and they cause climate change. Thankfully, our world has **renewable energy** that's better for the environment and will never run out. Earth's mix of renewable energy is reliable, easy to harness, and produces less waste than fossil fuels.

> The energy Earth receives from one hour of sunshine is around the same as the total amount of energy everyone on Earth uses in a year.

Solar panels

Solar power

Solar panels collect energy from the **sun** and turn it into electricity.

Wind
turbine

Blades

Wind power
Wind turbines get energy from
the **wind**. When the wind
blows, the blades turn and
they spin a generator that
produces electricity.

Hydroelectric dam

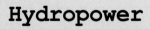

Hydropower
The energy of **water
moving** in rivers, oceans,
or lakes can turn turbines to
produce electricity. Dams are often
used to control the water flow.

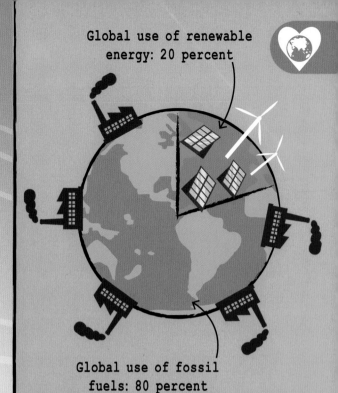

Global use of renewable
energy: 20 percent

Global use of fossil
fuels: 80 percent

Using renewables
Many countries are now choosing
to use renewable energy instead of
fossil fuels. Around **20 percent**
of global energy now comes from
renewable energy supplies.

Iceland produces all of
its energy from its
own renewable sources.

Iceland uses geothermal energy
(natural heat within Earth, which
is used to generate electricity)
and hydropower.

Green homes

There has never been a better time to go green! Here are some changes people can make at home to **help our planet**.

When you leave your home to go out, if possible don't travel by car. This helps to cut down on carbon dioxide being released into the air.

- **Install solar panels**.
- **Add roof insulation** to help keep heat in.

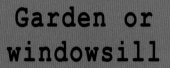

Garden or windowsill

- **Grow your own vegetables and fruit** so you buy less packaged food that has been transported.

Half of the world's carbon dioxide emissions come from

Living room

- **Turn off appliances** instead of leaving them on standby.
- **Switch off lights** when no one is in the room.

Bathroom

- **Have showers** instead of baths to limit water use.
- **Don't leave the tap running** when you brush your teeth.

Kitchen

- **Use reusable bags**.
- **Recycle** plastic, glass, cans, paper, and cardboard.
- **Make compost** from food waste and other compostable waste, if you can.

- **Grow plants** to absorb carbon dioxide, release oxygen, and create wildlife habitats.

only 11 percent of the population.

Pollution

Airplanes cause air and noise pollution.

Pollution happens when **harmful materials** are added to the environment. Different types of pollution threaten the health and happiness of all living things.

Pollution levels

The world is more polluted than ever before. **Towns** and **cities expand** as populations grow. **Factories** are built, **vehicles** fill the roads, **machines** are used, and **waste** piles up.

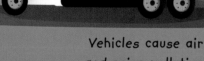
Vehicles cause air and noise pollution.

BEEP!
BEEP!

DRRRRRR!

Noisy construction

Noise pollution

Noise pollution is caused by such things as **whirring machinery**, **vehicles**, and **cell phones**. It creates disturbances and can lead to stress, lack of sleep, and hearing problems.

Light pollution

Street lights, **building lights**, and **flashing signs** upset human sleep patterns and impact our health. Artificial light is bad for many other animals too, and affects their behavior. Light pollution also makes it hard for astronomers to observe space.

Air pollution

Our air is polluted by **fumes** from **industries**, **heating**, and **cars**. The harmful gases make our planet hotter. They can also make people develop breathing problems.

Toxic chemicals

Soil pollution

Chemicals from industries and farms can leak into soil. They stop crops and other plants from growing, and animals can be harmed or killed.

Water pollution

Rivers, lakes, and oceans can be polluted by **waste products** such as **chemicals** and **human sewage**. As a result, one in three people around the world do not have access to safe drinking water.

Industrial waste water

199

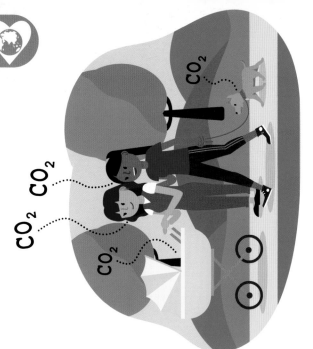

Carbon footprints

Your carbon footprint is not an actual footprint you leave in the ground. It's the total amount of **carbon dioxide (CO_2)** released into the atmosphere from your **lifestyle** over a period of time.

Carbon dioxide

Many things we do release the gas carbon dioxide, including **breathing out**, **heating homes**, and **driving cars**. This is causing problems for our planet.

Carbon footprint

It is hard to know exactly how much carbon dioxide we each create, but we can figure out an **estimate**. Knowing the amount helps us change our habits and reduce our carbon footprints.

Transportation

Traveling by car increases our carbon footprint.

Heating

Heating buildings adds to our footprint.

In the United States, an average person's carbon footprint for a year (the amount of carbon dioxide they release in a year) can weigh more than seven large cars.

Electricity

Using electrical equipment makes our carbon footprint bigger.

Aviation

Flights add to our carbon footprint.

Waste

Garbage stacks up in landfill sites, increasing our footprint.

Food

Food production is a major source of our carbon footprint.

Small steps

There are many ways you can **reduce** your carbon footprint, such as reusing things to waste less, vacationing closer to home, and walking or cycling whenever possible.

Bigfoot countries

Wealthy countries have a big carbon footprint. In wealthy countries, people create **more carbon dioxide** by buying, consuming, wasting, and traveling more than people in poorer nations.

The plastic problem

There is no doubt that plastic is fantastic. Just think of all the plastic products you use. The problem is **what happens to the plastic** once you've finished with it…

Rising use of plastic

Made from **oil**, plastic is **strong** and **cheap** to produce. Plastic use is on the rise—particularly because we buy a lot of plastic things, then throw them away.

Plastic waste

Plastic litter problem

Most plastic **doesn't break down** for hundreds of years. For example, a plastic bottle will break down after around 450 years. Since plastic takes so long to disintegrate, it builds up in landfill sites, oceans, and rivers.

Around 20,000 plastic bottles are bought every second, but less than half of them are recycled.

By 2050, scientists expect there will be

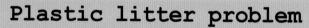

Bioplastics

Bioplastics can be made from **plant material**, such as wood chip or plant food waste. They can break down more quickly than most plastics made from oil. But bioplastics can still cause environmental problems, such as ocean pollution, and they cannot easily be recycled, so they are **not a perfect solution** to the plastic problem.

Wood chip   Bioplastic fork

SAFETY NOTE: Always wear protective gloves when you pick up litter.

Microplastics in the sea

Microplastics

When oil-based plastics and even some bioplastics do finally break down, they **don't totally decay**. They become **tiny pieces**, called microplastics. Creatures eat the pieces and pass them through the food chain to other animals, including humans.

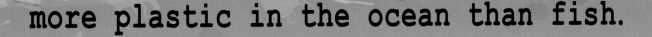

more plastic in the ocean than fish.

Cleaning up the oceans

Millions of tons of **plastic waste** is in our oceans. Thankfully, many people are helping to **clean it up**— and you can join them!

Plastic in the sea

Plastic in the oceans causes **great harm to sea life**. Most of it begins as **litter on land**. It is carried to the sea by streams and rivers.

Sea turtles can get caught in pieces of discarded fishing nets.

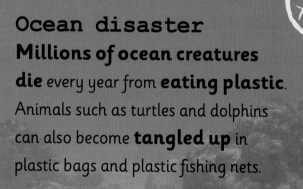

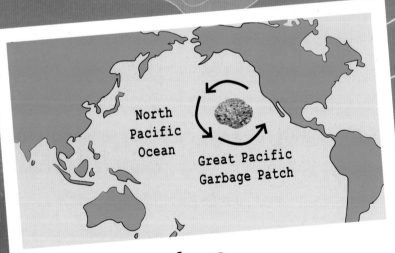

North Pacific Ocean

Great Pacific Garbage Patch

A sea of garbage

The biggest expanse of trash, called the **Great Pacific Garbage Patch**, is in the North Pacific Ocean. Trapped by ocean currents, it covers an area around one-sixth the size of the US.

Ocean disaster

Millions of ocean creatures die every year from **eating plastic**. Animals such as turtles and dolphins can also become **tangled up** in plastic bags and plastic fishing nets.

In the Philippines in 2019, a whale was found with 88 lb (40 kg) of plastic in its tummy—that's around the same weight as sixty basketballs.

Saving the seas

Here are **three ways** people are trying to clean our oceans.

1 **The Ocean Cleanup** organization is helping to remove the plastic in the world's oceans. Its cleanup system uses boats to tow a huge sheet of netting that collects the waste.

Ocean Cleanup system

The waste is returned to land for recycling.

SAFETY NOTE: Remember to wear protective gloves when you pick up litter.

2 The "**Take 3 for the Sea**" project encourages people to pick up three pieces of trash whenever they leave a beach.

Thank you!

The netting is open at the bottom so fish can escape.

3 Organized beach cleanups, such as **International Coastal Cleanup Day**, help to remove plastic waste that has been washed up on the shore.

Grow your own

Whether you've got a greenhouse, a garden, or a windowsill, you can grow your own food. It's a **fun** thing to do and it also helps the **planet!**

Homegrown

Homegrown food cuts down on the use of **transportation** and **plastic** because it doesn't need to be shipped or flown to stores in plastic containers. It also reduces the use of **farm chemicals** that can harm the environment.

Tasty tomatoes

Follow these steps to grow some **delicious tomatoes**.

Dig the ground to loosen the soil, and remove any weeds. Or fill a big pot with compost.

Sprinkle tomato seeds onto the soil, spacing them around 20 in (50 cm) apart.

Cover the seeds with a thin layer of soil and compost.

Waste not, want not

Each year, nearly half of the world's fruit and vegetables are wasted. If you can't eat everything you grow, **share it** with friends and neighbors.

CO_2

CO_2

CO_2

If you plant a tree, it will absorb carbon dioxide (CO_2), reducing climate change.

CO_2

CO_2

Grow your tomatoes in direct sunlight.

Water the seeds every day.

As the plants grow, add tomato food to their water.

When the tomatoes turn red, they are ready to eat!

Save our trees!

Trees are incredible. They **absorb harmful gases** and **provide homes** for plants and animals. But humans **cut down billions of them** every year to make use of their wood or to clear land.

Logging

Trees are chopped down for their **wood**. Tree logs are cut and used in buildings and furniture. Wood is also pulped to make paper, and burned as fuel.

Need for land

Many forests are cut down **so the land can be used**. Where the forests once were, people **keep animals**, **grow crops**, or **construct buildings**.

Cleaning the air

Trees take in **carbon dioxide** (**CO$_2$**). Like other plants, they release **oxygen** (**O$_2$**). Cutting down trees adds to climate change because those trees would have absorbed harmful carbon dioxide.

CO$_2$

CO$_2$

O$_2$

O$_2$ O$_2$

CO$_2$

Wildlife homes

As **forests disappear**, plants and animals lose their homes. It's becoming hard for orangutans to survive because their rainforest homes are being cut down to grow oil palm trees for palm oil.

To the rescue!

Protecting forests

People are working to protect forests by making them conservation areas. Once a forest is made a conservation area, no one is allowed to chop it down.

Planting trees

We can plant trees to replace those that have been cut down. However, these trees will take many years to become full-grown.

Shampoo

Bread

Palm oil is used in many day-to-day items, such as bread, cookies, and shampoo.

Palm oil

Ask family members to choose products that don't contain palm oil or products that use sustainable palm oil—palm oil that's grown without rainforests being cut down.

Cookies

209

That's **garbage!**

The enormous amount of trash we are throwing away is **harming our planet**. It's time to **take action** to reduce waste!

Millions of tons of waste are thrown away every day. I weigh a ton, so that's the same weight as millions of walruses like me!

Whopper waste

With nearly eight billion people living on Earth, **a lot of garbage** is produced. This includes everything from food waste and packaging to broken electronics and old clothes.

Incineration plant

Following the waste

After you throw garbage away, it gets taken to a **landfill site**, or an **incineration plant** where it is burned. Trash that we recycle is taken to **recycling plants**, where it is sorted and sent off to be used again.

Garbage problems

Incineration plants and landfill sites **produce air pollution, destroy the environment**, and **add to climate change**.

Dropping litter harms me and my friends. Animals can die from eating garbage or getting caught up in it, and litter also pollutes our habitats.

Recycle things and turn food waste into compost.

Reuse and recycle

The most common types of waste are **plastics**, **metals**, **glass**, **paper**, **clothes**, and **food**. But many of these materials can be reused or recycled. Before we throw things away, we should check if they can be **fixed**, **mended**, or **used again**.

Pass on clothes you no longer wear.

Try to fix things instead of throwing them away.

Recycling

Garbage can be **transformed** by the recycling process. Items such as cans, bottles, jars, plastic containers, paper, or cardboard are **broken down**, ready to be made into something **new**.

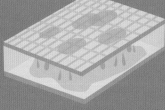

Paper recycling

Recycling paper uses **70 percent less energy** than making it new, and saves trees from being cut down. Here's how it's done.

Water is added to the paper to create a substance called slurry.

The slurry is mixed with chemicals and passed through screens. This removes stains and ink.

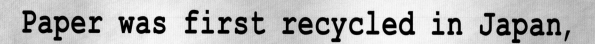

Paper was first recycled in Japan,

212

Recycling symbol

When you see this **symbol on an item**, it means that item can be recycled. So look out for it, and recycle whenever you can.

Bird feeder

Painted table

New bag

Upcycling

Giving old things a creative makeover is an alternative to recycling. You could paint an old table in rainbow colors, turn a plastic bottle into a bird feeder, or change an old pair of jeans into a new bag.

Air bubbles are used to remove any remaining ink. The ink sticks to the bubbles and they float to the surface, where they can be removed.

The slurry goes through more screens to remove things such as glue or staples, creating clean pulp.

The pulp is bleached white, then spread out and pressed to remove water. Once dry, it becomes a new sheet of paper that's ready to be rolled or cut, and used again.

more than 3,000 years ago.

Conservation

Many habitats and animals are under threat due to the actions of people. It is up to us to **look after our planet** and preserve it for future generations.

Forests provide habitats for thousands of species, and produce around one-third of Earth's oxygen (ocean plants produce the rest of our oxygen).

Saving our planet

Conservation is the act of **protecting** our world. For instance, turning **forests** into conservation areas stops them from being cut down to make space for farms or buildings.

The oceans are home to around one million species, and ocean plants produce roughly two-thirds of Earth's oxygen.

Ocean conservation

Oceans are damaged by overfishing, climate change, and pollution, including oil spills. Marine Protected Areas (MPAs) are parts of the ocean where fishing and other human activities are controlled to protect sea life.

Animal protection

Climate change and habitat destruction is harming wildlife. Animals are also hunted. For instance, people hunt rhinos for their horns, and elephants for their tusks. Hunting bans are one way we can save animals from extinction.

Animal reintroduction

Zoo breeding and reintroduction programs can increase animal populations. One such program saved the Arabian oryx. In 1972, it was classed as extinct in the wild, but now there are more than one thousand wild Arabian oryx.

Ecotourism

Ecotourism is environmentally friendly tourism. Businesses provide vacations that don't harm the environment, and money from the vacations helps local people and nature areas. This type of tourism can support conservation efforts.

What **can I do**?

The actions of one person can really **make a difference** and benefit our whole planet. We can all play a part by introducing **small changes**.

Grow some vegetables or fruit to reduce the use of food transportation and packaging.

Create wild spaces
Grow plants on your window ledge, balcony, or in your garden to create a habitat for insects.

Don't drop litter
Never be a litterbug! Always put your garbage **in the trash can** or **recycling bin**. You could also clean up littered areas—but make sure to wear protective gloves.

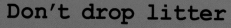

Find your voice

Share what you've learned with friends and family. Talk to your classmates, so they can join you in helping the planet. You could even give a talk at school to help spread the word.

Recycle

Recycle whatever you can, whether you're at home or out and about. Every item recycled is **one less in the landfill**.

Layer up or use the sun!

When the weather cools down, **put on an extra layer** instead of turning the heat on. And when the sun comes out, **dry clothes on a clothesline** instead of in a tumble dryer.

Reuse

Try to avoid using disposable plastic items. For instance, you could fill a **reusable bottle** with water instead of buying water in plastic bottles, and find a **shopping bag to use again and again**.

Today, around eighty countries have a full or partial ban on plastic bags.

Earth words

This book is filled with words about geography. Some can be a little tricky, so if you ever get stuck, look here.

Adapt When an animal or plant adapts, it changes over time to help it survive in its environment.

Air pressure The force of the air pressing down on an area.

Ancestors People from the past whom we are distantly related to.

Axis An imaginary line through an object, around which the object spins.

Climate change Changes to Earth's climate, particularly the changes caused by carbon dioxide and other gases in the atmosphere.

Continent A big area of land; most continents are made up of several countries.

Deciduous A deciduous plant loses its leaves in fall.

Electric charge Particles or objects have electric charge and can attract or repel each other; lightning is caused by particles attracting.

Environment Everything surrounding a living thing, including air, water, land, and other living things.

Equator An imaginary line that goes around the middle of Earth, halfway between the North Pole and the South Pole.

Evaporate When a liquid evaporates, it changes into a gas; water vapor is a gas.

Evergreen An evergreen plant keeps its leaves all year round.

Extinct When a plant or animal is extinct, it has died out and no longer exists on Earth; when a volcano is extinct, it is not expected to erupt in the future.

Fossil fuels Fuels formed from the remains of ancient plants and animals.

Gas A usually invisible substance, such as air, water vapor, or carbon dioxide.

Geography The study of places, including such things as Earth's landscapes, oceans, climate, and habitats, and how people live across the world.

Glacier A glacier is a gigantic mass of very slowly moving land ice that builds up over hundreds of years.

Habitat An environment where an animal or plant naturally lives.

Ice cap A thick layer of ice and snow permanently covering a land area; ice caps cover the polar regions.

Ice shelf A mass of ice floating on the sea that is connected to land ice.

Industrial Revolution When there were big changes in the way products were made in Europe and the US in the 1700s and 1800s; machines were invented and factories were built.

Industry In industries, people collect raw materials such as coal, make products to sell, or sell services.

Lava Hot, liquid rock that flows from a volcano.

Mineral A solid, naturally formed substance.

Nutrients Substances that help living things grow.

Particle A fragment, or an extremely small part of a solid, liquid, or gas.

Polar regions The areas at or near the North Pole and the South Pole.

Pollution Something that happens when harmful materials are added to the environment.

Population The number of living things in an area.

Predator An animal that hunts and kills other animals for food.

Prey Animals that are eaten by predators.

Primary Something that is primary is the most important or very important.

Species A group of plants or animals that share similar features and can breed together.

Sulphurous Something that contains or comes from a substance called sulphur.

Tectonic plates Large sections of Earth's surface, which move very slowly.

Temperature How hot or cold something is.

Toxic waste Waste that is harmful to living things.

Tropical Something from or related to areas near the equator, called the tropics.

Water vapor Very tiny drops of water in the air that you can't see; water vapor is a gas.

Index

Acknowledgments

DK would like to thank: Polly Goodman for proofreading; Helen Peters for compiling the index.

The publisher would like to thank the following for their kind permission to reproduce their photographs:

(Key: a=above; b=below/bottom; c=center; f=far; l=left; r=right; t=top)

1 123RF.com: Kittipong Jirasukhanont (tr). **Dorling Kindersley:** Holts Gems (bc); Natural History Museum, London (bc/Rose Quartz). **Dreamstime.com:** Dekanaryas (bc/Globe); Flowerstock (cra); Photopips (cr); Daniel Drobik (cr/helmet). 2 123RF.com: lattesmile (bl, bc/fishes). **Dorling Kindersley:** Oxford University Museum of Natural History (bc/Pumice). **Dreamstime.com:** Burlesck (bc, bc/sea creatures); Earnesttse (ca); Henner Damke (br). **Shutterstock.com:** Eva Speshneva (cb). 2–3 Dreamstime.com: Metelsky25 (a). 3 123RF.com: lattesmile (bc). **Dreamstime.com:** Bogadeva1983 (cr); Miceking (tl); Ruslan Minakryn (ca); Ssstocker (ca/Scavengery); Mansum008 (cb); Burlesck (bc/bottle); Smeshinka (bc/Fish); Elxeneize (br). 4 123RF.com: Alexey Sholom (crb). **Dreamstime.com:** Dima1970 (bl); Godruma (tr); Sylvia Lim (cla); Achmat Jappie (fcrb). 4–5 123RF.com: filmfoto (b). 5 Dreamstime.com: (br); Nguyen Phuong (bl); Roman Prysiazhniuk (tc); Artem Globenko (tr); QualitDesign (bc); Sabelskaya (bc/Cyclist). Getty Images / iStock: Antagain (cra). 6 123RF.com: filmfoto (b). **Dreamstime.com:** Lexiclaus (cla); Passakorn Umpornmaha (tr). **Getty Images / iStock:** Joesboy. 7 Dreamstime.com: (b); Oleg Seleznev (fbl); Evren Kalinbacak (bl); Ryan Fletcher (cb); Perfume316 (br). 8 Dorling Kindersley: Oxford University Museum of Natural History (bl). **Dreamstime.com:** Olga Samorodova (c); Vlad3563 (clb). **Getty Images / iStock:** epantha (crb). 9 Dorling Kindersley: Natural History Museum, London (bc/Rose Quartz). **Dreamstime.com:** Mansum008 (cr); Sergey Uryadnikov / Surz01 (cl); Gordon Tipene (br). **Fotolia:** apttone (bc). 10 Dreamstime.com: Emicristea (bc). 10–11 Dreamstime.com: (c). 11 Dreamstime.com: Viktarm (c). 12–13 Dreamstime.com: Pavel Rodimov. 12 Dreamstime.com: Roberto Atzeni (cr); Scol22 (tr). 13 123RF.com: Kittipong Jirasukhanont (cr). **Dreamstime.com:** Francisco Javier Ramos Rosellon (clb). 14 Dreamstime.com: Celia Ascenso (tr); Pavel Lapkouski (bl). 14–15 Dreamstime.com: Aghidel (b). 15 Dreamstime.com: Pavel Rodimov. 17 123RF.com: solarseven (crb). **Dreamstime.com:** Vladimir Kolosov (bl); Chumphon Whangchom (tl). 18–19 Dreamstime.com: 7xpert (c); ArtDesignWorks (Background). 20 Dorling Kindersley: Bob Gathany (cra). **Dreamstime.com:** Sebastian Kaulitzki (cl). 20–21 Dreamstime.com: Kulyk (c); David Woods (b). 21 Dorling Kindersley: NASA (tr). **Dreamstime.com:** Lineartestpilot (crb). 22–23 Dreamstime.com: 7xpert (ca); Mihai Andritoiu (b). 22 Dreamstime.com: (bc). 23 Dreamstime.com: Brian Shephard (crb); Vladimir Zadvinskii / Vldmr (br). 24–25 Dreamstime.com: Pavel Rodimov. 25 Dreamstime.com: Roberto Atzeni (c); Mansum008 (cra). **Shutterstock.com:** Aleksandr Pobedimskiy (tr). 26 Getty Images / iStock: Sjo (cr). 27 Dreamstime.com: Roberto Atzeni (cl); Jeanninebryan (r); Olga Samorodova (bc). **Getty Images / iStock:** PawelG Photo (l). 28 Dreamstime.com: Mansum008. 28–29 Dreamstime.com: Blueringmedia (t). 29 Dreamstime.com: Mansum008 (bl, crb); Daniel Prudek (cr). 32 123RF.com: lattesmile (c). **Dreamstime.com:** Fotofjodor (c/Fish); Seaphotoart (cl); Seadam (cb). **Shutterstock.com:** Eva Speshneva (cb). 32–33 Dreamstime.com: Seadam (c); Vrozhko (b). 33 123RF.com: Tung Pek Lean (c). **Alamy Stock Photo:** Jaime Franch Wildlife Photo (crb). **Dreamstime.com:** Kharlamova (cl).

35 Dorling Kindersley: NASA (br). **Dreamstime.com:** Ekaterina Brazhnikova (fbr); THPStock (t). 36 Dreamstime.com: Shunga_Shanga (cr); Sema Srinouljan (t). 37 Dreamstime.com: Shawn And Sue Roberts (c/girl); Sema Srinouljan (c); Siraphol (tl). 38–39 Dreamstime.com: Zoom-zoom (t). 39 Dreamstime.com: Luciano Mortula (c); Ssstocker (cra, cr); Vrozhko (br). 40 Dreamstime.com: Sebastian Kaulitzki (clb). 40–41 123RF.com: Aleksandr Frolov. **Dreamstime.com:** Mansum008 (c). 41 Dreamstime.com: Jose Gil / Joeygil (br); THPStock (bl); Sharon Jones (crb). **Getty Images / iStock:** thopson (cra). **Shutterstock.com:** Steve Bower (cr). 42–43 Dreamstime.com: Esebene. 43 Dreamstime.com: Andrea Muscatello (cr); Enrico Della Pietra (br). **Shutterstock.com:** Darryl Brooks (tc). 44–45 123RF.com: djapart (b). 44 Dreamstime.com: Mikhail Dudarev (crb); Mansum008 (tl). 45 Dreamstime.com: Ekaterina Lutokhina (cb/diamonds); Daniel Turbasa (cb). **Shutterstock.com:** Thorir Ingvarsson (t); iniaz (ca). 46–47 Dreamstime.com: Luckyphotographer. 47 Dreamstime.com: Ecelop (clb); Dmitry Islentyev (cra); Tearswept (br). 48 123RF.com: Rob Cicchetti (bl). 48–49 Dreamstime.com: THPStock (tr). 48–49 123RF.com: videowokart (cb). **Dreamstime.com:** Geografika (bc); Zoom-zoom. 49 Dorling Kindersley: Blueringmedia (cb); Tanaonte (tc); Samart Boonprasongthan (r). **Shutterstock.com:** JLStock (cra/Moon). 50–51 Dreamstime.com: George Burba. 51 Alamy Stock Photo: Alasdair Turner / Cavan Images (crb). **Dreamstime.com:** THPStock (c). 52–53 Dreamstime.com: Elxeneize (Peak); Zzvet (bl). 53 Dreamstime.com: Astankov Dmitry (br); Scattoselvaggio (bl); Zzvet (c). 54 Dorling Kindersley: Oxford University Museum of Natural History (crb). **Dreamstime.com:** Juliengrondin (c). **Shutterstock.com:** JLStock (clb). 55 Alamy Stock Photo: WidStock (tl). **Dorling Kindersley:** Sedgwick Museum of Geology, Cambridge (tr). **Dreamstime.com:** Sergey Rusakov / F4f (bc); Noppadon Sangpeam (clb). **Getty Images / iStock:** petekarici (cr). 58 Dorling Kindersley: Natural History Museum, London (bc). **Dreamstime.com:** Teacherphoto Photo (tr); Vlad3563 (br/Amethyst). **Science Photo Library:** Javier Trueba / MSF (cl). 59 Dorling Kindersley: Holts Gems (bl); Oxford University Museum of Natural History (ca); Natural History Museum, London (cb). **Dreamstime.com:** Spyros Arsenis; Ruslan Minakryn (cra). **Fotolia:** apttone (bc). 60 Dreamstime.com: Daria Rybakova / Podarenka (tl); Gordon Tipene (br). 61 Dreamstime.com: 9500057 Canada Inc. (fbr); Judy Rothchild (tc, cla); Korenyugin52 (cr); Torsten Velden / Tvelden (bc); Kharlamova (br). 63 Dreamstime.com: THPStock (bc). 64 Dreamstime.com: Iryna Kazlova Airspa (cb); Avictorero (bl); Gordon Tipene (br). 64–65 Dreamstime.com: Beata Becla; Vrozhko (Sand). 65 Dreamstime.com: Cristiborda (c); Hai Huy Ton That (tr). 66 Dreamstime.com: Amadeustx (bl). 66–67 Dreamstime.com: Emicristea. 67 Dreamstime.com: Markus Gann (cb); Elena Yakusheva (t); Qiming Yao (bl). 68 Dreamstime.com: Alexey Pushkin (t). 68–69 Dreamstime.com: Igorj. 69 Dreamstime.com: Alexander Konoplyov (c). 70–71 Shutterstock.com: Kit Leong (t). 71 Dreamstime.com: Iinspiration (cr). 72 Dreamstime.com: Katerina Kovaleva (ca); Nattawut Sakit (ca/Corn plant); Rsooll (c); Pzaxe (cb). **Getty Images / iStock:** t_kimura (cra/Grass). 73 Getty Images / iStock: BrianAJackson (crb); t_kimura (clb). 74–75 Dreamstime.com: Rahneda (b). 75 Dreamstime.com: Polygraphus (br); Sonyaillustration (tl); Viktoriia Yatskina (crb). 76 Dreamstime.com: Pop Nukoonrat (l). 77 Getty Images / iStock: JohnnyLye (bc). 78 Dreamstime.com: Erix2005 (bl). 79 Dreamstime.com: Michelle Bridges (cla); Cosmopol (bl). 80 Dreamstime.com: Dragoneye (bl). **Shutterstock.com:** Nicolaj Larsen (clb).

81 Dreamstime.com: Bennymarty (cr); Sararoom (cl). 82–83 Dreamstime.com: Blueringmedia (t). 82 Dreamstime.com: Astrid Gast (bc); Daria Rybakova / Podarenka (cr); Ginger Sanders (br). 83 Dreamstime.com: Craig Doros (bc); Eknarin Maphichai (t); Serban Enache (br). 84–85 Dreamstime.com: Yehuda Bernstein (t); Nicku (b); Blueringmedia (Background). 84 Dreamstime.com: Daniel Drobik (br). 85 Dreamstime.com: Lazarevael (r). 86 Dreamstime.com: Judy Rothchild (tr). 86–87 Dreamstime.com: Heizel (Background). 87 Dreamstime.com: Borlili (br); Sbelov (br). 88–89 Dreamstime.com: Metelsky25 (b). 89 Dorling Kindersley: Jerry Young (cla). **Dreamstime.com:** Roman Ivaschenko (fcra); Secondshot (cra/Anemone Fish). **Getty Images:** Sjoerd Bosch (tl). 90–91 Dreamstime.com: Sonerbakir. 91 Dorling Kindersley: Jerry Young (cla). **Dreamstime.com:** Rebecca Picard (clb). 92 Alamy Stock Photo: John Michaels (cb). **Dreamstime.com:** Denis Burdin (r); Kharlamova (b). 92–93 Dreamstime.com: Noppakun Wiropart (cb). 93 Courtesy of Nakheel: (crb). **Dreamstime.com:** Martinmark (tr); Ian Woolcock (clb). 94 Dreamstime.com: Rodrigolab (cl). 94–95 123RF.com: epicstockmedia (t). **Dreamstime.com:** Vrozhko (b). 95 Dreamstime.com: Chrisp543 (cra). **Shutterstock.com:** Maks Narodenko (tl). 96 Dreamstime.com: 9500057 Canada Inc. (bl); Ssstocker (cla); David Woods (cl); Korenyugin52 (bc); Cat Vec (br). 96–97 Dreamstime.com: Dedmazay. 98 Dreamstime.com: Artem Globenko; Jezper (l); Sabelskaya (bl); Pavlo Syvak (cb); Macrovector (cra). 98–99 Dreamstime.com: Nalaka Siriwardhana (cla); Miceking (cb). 99 Dreamstime.com: Guillermain (cla); Miceking (bc). **Shutterstock.com:** yukimco (br). 100 Dreamstime.com: Cbork7 (bc); Hpbfotos (br); Miceking (tr). 101 123RF.com: Adrian Hillman (cl). **Dreamstime.com:** Darinafis (br); Alexey Izotov (bl); Teh Soon Huat (bc). 102 Shutterstock.com: 22Images Studio (r). 102–103 Dreamstime.com: Zoom-zoom (t). 104 Dreamstime.com: Mitar Vidakovic (tl). 105 Dreamstime.com: Andrei Calangiu (crb); Darkmonk (ca); Rangizzz (cra); Photomailbox (bl). 107 Dreamstime.com: Ivan Burchak (t); Yulia Gapeenko (cr, br, fcr). 108 Dreamstime.com: Anna Gordeeva (r); Magicshapes (l); Guillermain (cra); Nalaka Siriwardhana (cb); Spacedrone808 (r/landscape). **Getty Images / iStock:** Gregory_DUBUS (bl). 109 Dreamstime.com: Beata Becla (l); Sabelskaya (bl); Arkadi Bojarinov (ftr); Lucila De Avila Castilho (tr); Handersonchulet (cr); Solaris Images Inc (crb). 110 Dreamstime.com: Ilya Fedoseev (c); Multipedia2014 (r). 110–111 Dreamstime.com: Ilya Fedoseev (tc); Olga Kurbatova; Ominaesi (Rain). 111 Dreamstime.com: Rijal Muttaqin (clb); Seamartini (ca); Pavel Naumov (ca/Chinese Farmer); Michael Williams (br). 112–113 Dreamstime.com: Guillermain; Nalaka Siriwardhana (Snow flakes); Maxborovkov (Background). 112 Dreamstime.com: Alexandr Kazanskiy (tl); Roman Prysiazhniuk (t); Onepony (br). 113 Alamy Stock Photo: Fred Olivier / Nature Picture Library (tc). **Dreamstime.com:** Martingraf (bl); Dan Ross (crb). **Shutterstock.com:** yukimco (cr). 114–115 Dreamstime.com: Iulius Costache; Niagaragirl (Background). 114 Dreamstime.com: Kelpfish (cl). 115 Dreamstime.com: Nastiakonko19 (cr); Stnazkul (cla). 116–117 Dreamstime.com: Kvmilju. 116 Dreamstime.com: Larry Rains (br); THPStock. 117 Dreamstime.com: Pixelappeal (cb). 118 Dreamstime.com: Jezper (bc, r). 118–119 123RF.com: filmfoto (b). **Dreamstime.com:** Zoom-zoom. 119 Dreamstime.com: Bogadeva1983 (tc); Vladimir Ivanov (c); THPStock (br). 120 Dreamstime.com: Topgeek (cla). 120–121 Dreamstime.com: Justin Hobson; Igor Zubkov (tornado). 121 123RF.com: Darko Komorski / kommaz (bc). **Dreamstime.com:** Sabelskaya. 122 Dreamstime.com: Artem Globenko (bl); Maksym Kapliuk (cra). 122–123 Dreamstime.com: Artem Globenko (bc); Anuwat Meereewee (wave). 123 Dreamstime.com: Tuksaporn Rattanamuk (r); Xneo (cla).